Hands-On Computing: Using WordPerfect 5.1

R. Dale Hobart
Sharon Octernaud
Sid Sytsma
Ferris State University

Macmillan Publishing Company
New York
Collier Macmillan Canada, Inc.
Toronto
Maxwell Macmillan International Publishing Group
New York Oxford Singapore Sidney

Cover photo: Larry Hamill

Editor: Vernon R. Anthony

Cover Designer: Brian Deep

This book was set using Aldus PageMaker® with LaserMaster® ITC Bookman, Sans, Symbols, and Courier type. Screen captures made with HiJaak®.

Printed in the United States of America

Macmillan Publishing Company
866 Third Avenue, New York, New York 10022

Collier Macmillan Canada, Inc.

Library of Congress Catalog Card Number: 90-64084
International Standard Book Number: 0-675-22374-1

Printing: 2 3 4 5 6 7 8 9 Year: 2 3 4

Preface

Introduction

Microcomputers are becoming an accepted part of American life. They are found in homes, in schools, in businesses, and in industry. The $1,000 microcomputer system of today has the computing power of a $1,000,000 mainframe computer of twenty years ago. And the revolution has just begun!

This series is designed to assist people in learning how to use the microcomputer as a tool. The concept and materials were developed by the authors as a result of numerous "hands-on" computer literacy workshops given for the faculty and staff of Ferris State University.

The Philosophy of the Series

Many technical computer science and data processing books have been written. Their emphases lie in describing how a computer works and in teaching the use of a computer language. This series describes **how to use** a microcomputer. Step-by-step exercises illustrate spreadsheet, word processing, data management, and telecommunication tasks.

This series is not designed to be read from cover to cover. Beginning with Chapter 2 in the MS-DOS series, the learner is expected to be an active participant working through the tutorial exercises at an IBM or compatible microcomputer.

The Software Used in this Series

Several widely used software packages are explained in this series. The word processing programs, **WordPerfect 5.1**, **WordStar 5.5**, and **Microsoft Word for DOS 5**, are among the most popular full-featured word processors in use today. The electronic spreadsheet program **Lotus 2.2** is frequently employed in the business world. The data file management programs **dBASE IV**, **FoxPro**, and **Paradox 3** are designed for professionals and are easy to use. The **ProComm Plus** communications program is fast and simple to use.

Organization of the Series

This series is organized in a modular fashion. Each module can be studied independently with a minimum amount of introductory material. Each program can be explored at a beginning, intermediate, or advanced level. However, the introductory MS-DOS module should be studied before any of the program modules are used. When teaching microcomputer applications to computer novices, the authors have found that introducing spreadsheet features, then word processing concepts, followed by data base management characteristics to be the most successful instructional sequence.

Equipment and Setup Requirements

To use the programs in this book, the following equipment is needed:

IBM-PC or compatible with
- one floppy disk drive
- one hard disk
- 640K RAM
- a monitor
- a printer

To perform the telecommunications exercise, a modem is required.

This text assumes that the programs were installed according to the setup procedures in the software documentation with the recommended default settings.

Using the Exercise Disk

To reduce student typing time, several data files have been created for use with the intermediate and advanced exercises in this series. If any of these files are needed to complete a lesson, the introductory paragraphs of the exercises specify the file names. These files should be copied onto another formatted diskette to insure that the files on the *Exercise Disk* remain unchanged.

The *Exercise Disk* contains a subdirectory for each module in the series. The files from the appropriate subdirectory should be copied to the root directory of a floppy disk for use with the exercise. The exercise is written assuming that the files are in the root directory of a floppy diskette.

In some cases, files created by the user in a beginning or intermediate exercise are used in future lessons. Users should make backup copies of their working data diskettes to permit ready access to these files.

The *Exercise Disk* is available in the instructor's manual. For further details, contact your local Macmillan Publishing Company representative.

About the Authors

The authors work at Ferris State University in Big Rapids, Michigan. They are actively involved in creating and teaching microcomputer applications workshops and classes for the campus, business professionals, and educators around the state.

Dale Hobart is an attorney and former Program Director of the Paralegal Program at Ferris. In his role as Coordinator of Academic Computing, he specializes in solving computer-related problems of a technical nature and in teaching microcomputer applications to working adults.

Sharon Octernaud is a foreign language teacher and has worked with adults in providing instructional support for the blind. Currently she is the college Microcomputer Software Trainer and develops computer-related training materials for workshops.

Sid Sytsma is an engineer, formerly the Coordinator of Academic Computing, and currently the Assistant Vice-President for Academic Affairs at Ferris. Previously, he taught statistics in the Department of Computer Information Systems and received the *Distinguished Teacher of the Year Award.*

Contents

Introduction to Word Processing	**1**
Objectives	1
Defining Word Processing	1
Creating a Document	1
Editing a Document	2
Formatting and Printing a Document	2
Word Processing Applications	3
Spelling Checkers and Thesauruses	3
WordPerfect 5.1 Beginning Exercise	**5**
Objectives for the WordPerfect Beginning Exercise	5
Scope of the Exercise	5
Starting the Lesson	6
Loading WordPerfect	6
Entering Text	7
Accessing the Help Screens	7
Moving Around the Screen	9
Revising Text	10
Deleting Text	10
Inserting Text	11
Marking, Moving, and Copying Text	11
Copying Text	12
Moving Text	13
Deleting a Text Block	14
Restoring a Text Block	14
Searching for and Replacing Text	15
Changing Type Styles	16
Saving a Document	17
Printing a Document	18
Exiting WordPerfect	19
Conclusion	19
Practice Beginning WordPerfect	20
Beginning WordPerfect Projects	27
WordPerfect 5.1 Intermediate Exercise	**29**
Objectives for the WordPerfect Intermediate Exercise	29
Scope of the Exercise	29
Starting the Lesson	29
Loading WordPerfect	30
Margins and the Format Command	30
Centering Text	31
Format Command and Tabs	32
Using Tabs and Indents	35
Joining Files	36
The Format Command and Print Options	38
Line Spacing	38
Header and Footer Lines	39
Page Numbers	40
Pagination	42

Global Search and Replace 44
Deleting and Undeleting 45
Exiting WordPerfect 46
Conclusion 47
Practice Intermediate WordPerfect 48
Intermediate WordPerfect Projects 61

WordPerfect 5.1 Advanced Exercise **63**
Objectives for the WordPerfect Advanced Exercise 63
Scope of the Exercise 63
Starting the Lesson 63
Loading WordPerfect 64
Font Types Revisited 64
Text Format Codes 67
Master Documents 69
Footnotes 73
Indexing 75
Windows 79
Saving a Document and Exiting WordPerfect 81
Conclusion 82
Practice Advanced WordPerfect 83
Advanced WordPerfect Projects 89

WordPerfect 5.1 Spell Checking and Thesaurus Exercise **91**
Objectives for the Spell Checking and Thesaurus Exercise 91
Scope of the Exercise 91
Starting the Lesson 91
Loading WordPerfect 92
Spell Checking a Document 92
Using the Thesaurus 95
Exiting WordPerfect 97
Conclusion 97
Practice Using Spell Checking and the Thesaurus 98

Word Perfect 5.1 Mail Merge **99**
Objectives for Mail Merge 99
Defining Mail Merge 99

Word Perfect 5.1 Mail Merge Exercise **101**
Objectives for the Mail Merge Exercise 101
Scope of the Exercise 101
The Mail Merge Process 101
Starting the Lesson 102
Converting Files to a WordPerfect Format 102
Loading the CONVERT Program 103
Converting the File 103
Loading WordPerfect 105
Creating a Document for Mail Merging 105

The Secondary File 105
The Primary File 106
Merging the Secondary File with the Letter 112
Printing the Merged Document 114
Ending the Lesson 115
Conclusion 116
Mail Merge Projects 117

INDEX 119

Introduction to Word Processing
WordPerfect 5.1

Objectives

Learn how to:

1. Describe word processing.

2. Recognize situations where word processing would increase productivity.

3. Describe the four basic functions of word processing:

    a. creating a document,
    b. editing a document,
    c. formatting a document; and
    d. printing a document.

4. Describe the use of a spelling checker and a thesaurus.

5. Define and use the following terms:

    boilerplate
    mail merge
    spelling checker
    thesaurus
    word processing
    word wrap

Defining Word Processing

Word processing is the most frequently used microcomputer application. A word processor is used in place of a typewriter. Letters, memos, reports, briefs, and books are easier to prepare with a word processor than with a typewriter. Someone with limited typing skills can soon become a confident and competent typist when using a word processor. The steps involved when producing a document with a word processor parallel those of producing a document with a typewriter. Word processing consists of four basic functions: creating, editing, formatting, and printing.

Creating a Document

The difference between a typewriter and a word processor becomes apparent with the initial draft of a document. Characters typed on a typewriter appear on paper and characters typed on a computer appear on a monitor. Unlike a traditional typist, the computer user does not listen for a bell to indicate the end of a line because a word processor automatically moves a word down to the next line when the right margin is reached. The Enter key is pressed only to end a paragraph or to finish a short line.

Editing a Document

Editing with the computer is easier than editing with the typewriter. When a typing error is made at the computer keyboard, there is no need to use correction fluid. If a letter or sentence is left out, it can be inserted. If an incorrect letter is typed, the correct letter can be typed directly over the wrong one. If there are too many characters, the Delete key can be used to remove them. If editing affects paragraph alignment, realignment automatically occurs when the text is reformatted. The task of writing becomes infinitely easier.

This writer revises text on the screen prior to printing a hard copy. The word processing system is composed of a microcomputer, a printer, and a word processing program.

Text entry and editing are two of many ways to increase productivity through word processing. Once a document is entered into the computer, it can be used over and over again. Standard paragraphs can be saved, modified, and inserted as needed. Documents can be designed so that names can be entered once and automatically included at many different locations in the final output. A document can be rearranged by moving paragraphs and sentences. Large or small sections of text may be moved, deleted, or duplicated.

Formatting and Printing a Document

Word processing provides a large selection of printing and formatting options. These options include changing type styles and sizes, setting multiple margins, using right margin alignment, activating automatic page numbering, setting variable line spacing, creating page headers and footers, using footnotes, building a table of contents, and creating an index. Documents produced with these formatting tools can be attractive and professional in appearance.

Word Processing Applications

Word processing markedly increases productivity when large numbers of similar documents need to be produced. A letter can be merged with a mailing list, yielding a series of personalized letters. This process of joining a form letter with a data base is called mail merge.

When a document is written, often several revisions are needed before the final copy is produced. As editing can be accomplished easily with a word processor, text requiring extensive revision is a prime candidate for word processing. A standard document can be modified to reflect current data. Perhaps a date needs to be changed or a number on a price list updated. The document can be retrieved from disk, the changes made, and the document reprinted in minutes.

Frequently, documents consist of standard text plus custom text. Legal documents are of this type. The standard paragraphs are called "boilerplate." The document is tailored to a particular situation by inserting "boilerplate" paragraphs within a document containing customized text.

Spelling Checkers and Thesauruses

A spelling checker and a thesaurus are tools used in conjunction with a word processor to facilitate spelling and word selection. Most word processing programs, including WordPerfect, have a built-in spelling checker and thesaurus. Other software requires the use of an independent spelling checker and thesaurus program. An independent spelling checker and thesaurus program is loaded into the computer before any other program is used. Because it is an independent program, it can be used with applications other than word processing.

A spelling checker compares words in a document with those in a dictionary stored on disk. A variety of spelling checkers exists. The less complex programs place a mark on any word not contained in the program's dictionary, permitting the user to review and correct the marked words. More sophisticated spelling programs not only locate words not found in the computer's dictionary, but also present a list of several words that the misspelling could represent. Transposed letters easily overlooked by proofreaders are quickly discovered by running an electronic spell check. However, a spelling checker will not indicate that "to" has been typed when "two" or "too" should have been used, as all three of these words are spelled correctly.

A thesaurus provides a list of synonyms for a given word. To use an electronic thesaurus, the cursor is moved to any character within the word for which a synonym is desired. A designated function key is pressed and synonyms for the indicated word are displayed. A word is replaced by moving the cursor to the desired synonym and pressing the Enter key. The selected synonym replaces the target word within the document.

Five step-by-step word processing exercises are included in this module. The word processing tools explained in the Beginning Exercise will satisfy the needs of many users. Users requiring more sophisticated tools should progress to the Intermediate Exercise. A short exercise explaining the use of the spelling checker and thesaurus follows the Advanced Exercise but can be undertaken after completion of the Beginning Exercise. The final exercise demonstrates the use of the mail merge features of WordPerfect.

WordPerfect 5.1
Beginning Exercise

Objectives

Learn how to:

1. Load the WordPerfect word processing program into the computer.

2. Create a document with WordPerfect.

3. Access WordPerfect help screens.

4. Move around a document using the Home, End, PgUp, PgDn, and arrow keys.

5. Revise text material by

    a. inserting text,
    b. deleting text,
    c. marking, copying, and moving blocks of text,
    d. undeleting text; and
    e. searching for and replacing text.

6. Change type styles within WordPerfect.

7. Save a WordPerfect file to disk.

8. Print a document.

9. Exit WordPerfect.

Scope of the Exercise

This lesson describes how to load and use the word processing program WordPerfect. The topics covered include: loading the program, creating a document, entering text, modifying text, reformatting text, moving blocks of text, using the search and replace feature, changing type styles, saving a document, printing a document, and exiting the program.

Before starting this exercise, WordPerfect must be installed and a printer selected. If this has not been done, follow the instructions in the WordPerfect manual or consult your instructor, lab assistant, or the person who installed your software.

Starting the Lesson

For this lesson, everything to be typed at the keyboard is underlined and also appears in the margin. Text appearing on the computer's screen during the lesson is indicated in `courier type`.

Boot: the computer

1. Before the WordPerfect program can be used to turn a computer into a word processor, the operating system must be loaded into the computer. If a system prompt (C>, a menu, or something similar) is not displayed on the screen, follow the steps described in the Getting Started Exercise in the DOS module to boot the system.

Insert: data disk in drive A:

2. If you are using a hard drive system and the WordPerfect installation instructions have been followed, WordPerfect resides on the hard drive. Insert a formatted diskette into drive A:. The diskette in drive A: is the working data disk. Any files created during this lesson will be saved onto this disk.

   -or-

   If a computer with a different configuration is being used, ask your instructor or lab assistant for directions specific to your setup.

Loading WordPerfect

The computer must be provided with the instructions on how to be a word processor. This is done by loading the WordPerfect program into the computer's temporary memory (RAM). To load WordPerfect and to begin executing the program, complete the following steps.

Type: cd\wp51 <ENTER>
Type: wp

1. If you are using a hard drive, log into the WordPerfect subdirectory by typing CD\WP51 and pressing <ENTER>. Then, type WP. (Uppercase or lowercase may be used.)

   -or-

   If you are in a lab or network setting, verify the above commands with your instructor or lab assistant.

   WP is the command that tells MS-DOS to load the WordPerfect program into the computer and to start the program.

Press: <ENTER>

2. Execute the above command by pressing the <ENTER> key. The Enter key signals to the computer that the command has been completely typed and needs to be carried out.

   The Return key and Enter key, if the keyboard has both, are interchangeable. These exercises will use <ENTER> to indicate that either the Return key or Enter key is to be pressed.

Entering Text

A blank screen is displayed and the status line appears in the lower right corner of the monitor. This message indicates the current status of WordPerfect and should be similar to the line displayed below.

```
Doc 1 Pg 1 Ln 1" Pos 1"
```

This status line informs the user of the location of the cursor in the document. The **Doc 1** indicates that the cursor is located in document number 1. WordPerfect permits editing more than one document at a time. The **Pg 1** indicates that the cursor is on page one of the document. The **Ln 1**" indicates that the cursor is on a line one inch from the top of the page. The **Pos 1**" indicates that the cursor is in column position 1, one inch from the left edge of the page. The Ln and Pos information can be displayed in inches, centimeters, points (used by print shops), and WordPerfect units (lines and columns). WordPerfect can be configured to display the cursor location using any one of these units of measure.

When entering the four-sentence paragraph shown below, use the arrow keys to change the position of the cursor. Do not use the space bar as this would insert blank spaces in the text. The Del and Backspace keys are useful for erasing typing errors.

As text is typed, any word extending beyond the right margin is automatically moved down to the next line. This feature is called word wrap. When entering text, allow the computer to use the word wrap feature. A carriage return should not be inserted manually at the end of a line because WordPerfect moves text to a new line when the right margin is reached. However, to begin a new paragraph or to enter a short line, press the Enter key.

Your monitor may not display the same words at the end of the lines as those in the paragraph below. Line break locations are dependent upon the printer in use.

Key in the following text for use in this lesson.

When I first started to learn about personal computers, I did not like them very much. You might say that I hated them. I did not understand how they could be useful in an office and did not ever want to use one. Now that I am learning how to do word processing on a computer, I know that I hate them.

Type: the underlined text as shown at left

Accessing the Help Screens

WordPerfect has built-in help screens. These screens describe how to use various features of the program. The help screens can be activated by pressing the F3 key. After the initial help screen has been displayed, press the first letter of the desired help topic. An alphabetical listing of help topics then appears on the screen. If the topic is not shown on the screen, pressing the first letter of the topic again will display more of the list. A help topic is selected by pressing the designated key or key combination displayed on the monitor. Pressing the F3 key twice displays a function key template. Pressing the Enter key or the space bar terminates the help option and redisplays the document.

To obtain information on how text is moved, complete the following steps.

Press: F3

1. Press the F3 key to display the initial help screen.

   The screen displays

```
Help                                                    WP 5.1   01/19/90

     Press any letter to get an alphabetical list of features.

          The list will include the features that start with that letter,
          along with the name of the key where the feature is found.  You
          can then press that key to get a description of how the feature
          works.

     Press any function key to get information about the use of the key.

          Some keys may let you choose from a menu to get more information
          about various options.  Press HELP again to display the template.


Selection: 0                                        (Press ENTER to exit Help)
```

Type: M

2. Type M to display the help index for the letter m (Move Text).

   The Move Text feature does not appear in the alphabetized listing displayed on the screen.

Type: M twice

3. Type M twice to display the Move Text entry.

   The right column indicates that help for this feature is obtained by pressing the Ctrl-F4 key combination.

4. While holding down the Ctrl key, press the F4 key to display the Move Text help screen.

   The screen displays

```
Move

     Lets you move, copy or delete text.  You can then move to another place in
     the document or to a document in the second editing screen and retrieve
     the text.  You can also append a block of text to a file on disk.

     You must first highlight the text you want to move, copy, etc.  You can
     either use the Block feature to highlight the desired text, or let the
     Move key automatically highlight the current sentence, paragraph, or page.

     1 - Block On

     2 - Block Off






Selection: 0                                        (Press ENTER to exit Help)
```

Press: Ctrl-F4

5. Type 1 to display information about Block On.

   Explore other topics by pressing any key or key combination except for the Enter key or the space bar. Some of the help screens may not make much sense at this time. As WordPerfect and word processing terminology become more familiar, the screens will have greater meaning.

Type: 1

6. When you have completed your initial exploration of the help screens, press the <ENTER> key to redisplay the document.

Press: <ENTER>

Moving Around the Screen

The arrow keys are used to move the cursor around the screen one character or line at a time. The arrow keys are located on the right side of the keyboard. In some cases the arrow keys are part of the numeric keypad. On other keyboards, the arrow keys are separate from the numeric keypad.

Documents having more than 24 lines are too long to be shown in their entirety on the monitor. The up arrow key and down arrow key can be used to bring undisplayed text into view. Moving the cursor up when it is located at the top of the screen displays the preceding line of text on the top of the screen unless the first line of the document is already in view. Likewise, moving the cursor down past the bottom of the screen brings another line of text into view unless the cursor is positioned on the last line of the document.

The End key is located near the arrow keys. This key can be used to move the cursor to the end of a line. The Home key is also located near the arrow keys. Pressing the Home key followed by an arrow key moves the cursor to the edge of the screen. Thus, pressing the Home key followed by the left arrow key moves the cursor to the left of the screen. Pressing the Home key followed by the up, down, or right arrow keys moves the cursor to the top, bottom, or right edge of the screen.

Pressing the PgUp key or the PgDn key moves the displayed text backward or forward a screen at a time. Pressing the Home key twice followed by the up arrow or the down arrow key places the cursor at the beginning or at the end of a document. The WordPerfect manual and built-in help screens describe additional methods for quickly moving the cursor within a document.

Practice moving the cursor around the paragraph by using the arrow, Home, and End keys.

Revising Text

The ease of revising existing material is one of the greatest benefits of using a word processor. When a mistake is made in typewritten text, the entire document must be retyped. Mistakes in a document created with a word processor can be corrected on the screen and the entire document quickly reprinted.

Deleting Text

Text may be deleted and inserted. In the paragraph typed for this exercise, the phrase **personal computer** will be changed to **microcomputer**. To do this, the word **personal** needs to be deleted and the prefix **micro** needs to be inserted.

Personal could be deleted by placing the cursor at the letter **p** and pressing the Del key eight times. However, it would be more efficient to use a command that would delete an entire word.

To access the help feature to identify the command used to delete an entire word and to delete the word **personal** from the first line of the paragraph, complete the following steps.

Press: F3

1. Press the F3 key to display the initial help screen.

Type: D

2. To display information about the Delete Word feature, type D.

   The screen displays the beginning of the D listing. However, Delete Word is not displayed.

Type: D

3. Type D to display Delete Word. The screen displays the designated command as Ctrl-Bksp (Backspace).

4. While holding down the Ctrl key, press the Backspace key to view the Delete Word help screen.

   Press: Ctrl-Backspace

5. To return to the document, press the <ENTER> key.

   Press: <ENTER>

6. Using the arrow keys, position the cursor under the **p** in **personal**.

   Position cursor: under the p in personal

7. To delete the word **personal**, while holding down the Ctrl key, press the Backspace key.

   Press: Ctrl-Backspace

   The word **personal** is deleted from the screen.

Inserting Text

WordPerfect supports two text entry modes. The normal mode inserts characters at the cursor as they are typed and moves existing text to the right. The typeover mode replaces the character at the cursor with the newly typed character. The Insert key toggles WordPerfect between the normal and typeover modes.

Press the Ins key (located at the lower right of the keyboard) and notice that the left side of the status message line displays the word `Typeover` on the left side of the screen.

Press: Ins key

Press the Ins key again to change WordPerfect back to the normal mode.

Press: Ins key

Insert the prefix **micro** to replace the deleted word **personal** by completing the following steps.

1. If necessary, press the Ins key to turn typeover off.

   Verify: normal mode

2. If necessary, use the arrow keys to position the cursor directly under the **c** in the word **computers**.

   Position cursor: under the c in computers

3. Type micro to replace the deleted word personal. (Microcomputer is one word.)

   Type: micro

Marking, Moving, and Copying Text

While the method described on the previous page is useful when making minor changes to the text, it does not efficiently move, copy, or delete large portions of text. In word processing, a large section of text is called a block. Separate commands are used to mark portions of the document as blocks, enabling the user to copy, move, or delete them.

Copying Text

The block command is used to duplicate a portion of text at another location within a document. The location for the copied text can be on a new line, in the middle of a paragraph or sentence, or in the middle of a word. The original block is left unchanged. The help screen indicates that the Block command is executed by using the Alt-F4 key combination.

The cursor is moved to the first character of text to be copied, and the Alt-F4 key combination is pressed. Next, the cursor is positioned at the end of the text to be copied and the Ctrl-F4 key combination is pressed. This command marks the end of the block and displays a menu from which the 1 is selected to choose a Block move. Another menu is displayed and the user types 2 to select Copy. The last step in copying a block of text is to position the cursor at the location where the newly copied text is to be placed and to press the Enter key.

To copy the word **micro** before the word **computer** in the last sentence of the paragraph, complete the following steps.

Position cursor: under the m in micro
Press: Alt-F4

1. Using the arrow keys, position the cursor under the **m** of **micro**.

2. To mark the beginning of the text to be copied, press the Alt-F4 key combination.

   The status line displays the flashing words `Block on`.

Highlight: micro

3. To mark the word **micro**, press the right arrow key until the word **micro** has been highlighted.

Press: Ctrl-F4

4. To select the Move option, press the Ctrl-F4 key combination.

   The status line displays

   `Move: 1 Block; 2 Tabular Column; 3 Rectangle: 0`

Type: 1

5. To select a Block move, type 1.

   The status line displays

   `1 Move; 2 Copy; 3 Delete; 4 Append; 0`

Type: 2

6. To Copy the marked text, type 2.

   The status line displays

   `Move cursor; press Enter to retrieve.`

Position cursor: under the c in computer

7. Use the arrow keys to position the cursor under the **c** in the word **computer** in the last sentence of the paragraph.

8. To copy the marked text to the new location, press the <ENTER> key.

   Press: <ENTER>

   The word **microcomputer** now appears in the first sentence and in the last sentence of the paragraph.

Moving Text

The Move command is used to relocate a block of text within a document. This command is very useful when reorganizing text. The Move command is executed with the Ctrl-F4 key combination. The steps in the move process are similar to the steps in the copy process. However, 1 for Move is selected from the Move menu rather than 2 for Copy.

In this example, the Block command will not be used to mark a block before selecting the Move feature. When Move is selected without first marking a block, the text at the cursor may be chosen as a sentence, paragraph or page. The cursor is placed anywhere within the unit to be moved and the Ctrl-F4 key combination is pressed. Next, the desired unit is selected. The last step in moving a unit of text is to position the cursor at the location where the moved text is to be placed and to press the <ENTER> key.

To move the third sentence, **I did not understand how they could be useful in an office and did not ever want to use one.**, to the end of the paragraph, complete the following steps.

1. Using the arrow keys, position the cursor under any character in the third sentence, **I did not understand how they could be useful in an office and did not ever want to use one.**

   Position cursor: at any character in third sentence

2. To activate the Move command, press the Ctrl-F4 key combination.

   Press: Ctrl-F4

   The status line displays

   `Move: 1 Sentence; 2 Paragraph; 3 Page; 4 Retrieve: 0`

3. To indicate that the unit to be moved is a Sentence, type 1.

   Type: 1

   The sentence is highlighted and the status line displays

   `1 Move; 2 Copy; 3 Delete; 4 Append: 0`

4. To indicate the Move option, type 1.

   Type: 1

   The highlighted sentence disappears from the screen and the status line displays

   `Move cursor; press Enter to retrieve.`

Position cursor: two spaces after the last word of the paragraph

5. To place this sentence at the end of the document, use the arrow keys and space bar to position the cursor two spaces after the last word of the paragraph. (Typing standards require two spaces after a period at the end of a sentence.)

Press: <ENTER>

6. To place the sentence at the cursor location, press the <ENTER> key.

   After the move, this sentence appears only at the end of the document.

Correct: spacing problems

7. Examine the text and correct any spacing problems that may have occurred when the text was moved and the paragraph re-formatted.

Deleting a Text Block

The phrase **and did not ever want to use one** is not needed. Delete this phrase by completing the following steps.

Position cursor: under the a of and

1. Using the arrow keys, position the cursor under the **a** of **and** in the sentence located at the end of the paragraph.

Press: Alt-F4

2. Begin marking the block of text by pressing the Alt-F4 key combination.

   The status line displays the flashing words `Block on`.

Highlight: text to be deleted

3. Highlight the text to be deleted by moving the cursor to the end of the sentence by pressing the arrow keys.

Press: Backspace

4. To delete the text, press the Backspace key.

   The status line displays:

   `Delete Block? No (Yes)`

Type: Y

5. To delete the block, type Y.

Restoring a Text Block

In WordPerfect, pressing the F1 key activates the Cancel command. This feature is used to cancel the last Move or Block Delete action. To restore a deleted block of text, the cursor is positioned at the location of the erased material and the F1 key is pressed.

Deleting that last phrase was a mistake! To restore the deleted text, complete the following steps.

1. If necessary, use the arrow keys to position the cursor at the location of the deleted text.

   Position cursor: at location of deleted text

2. To Restore the text, press the F1 key.

   Press: F1

   The status line displays:

   ```
   Undelete:  1 Restore; 2 Previous Deletion:0
   ```

3. Type 1 to complete the Restore process.

   Type: 1

   The highlighting disappears from the screen.

Searching for and Replacing Text

The Search and Replace feature of WordPerfect scans a document for specified text and replaces that text with the designated characters. This feature is useful when correcting a spelling error or changing a date throughout an entire document.

The Search and Replace command is activated by pressing the Alt-F2 key combination. The desired search is specified by indicating with or without confirmation. Next, the text to be found is designated. Pressing the F2 key displays a request for the replacement text. The search is begun by pressing the F2 key. The search ends when the last occurrence of the indicated word or phrase has been encountered.

In this lesson, a serious mistake was made. The word **adore** should have been typed but somehow the word **hate** was entered! Use the Search and Replace function to correct this egregious error by changing the verb **hate** to **adore**.

1. To position the cursor at the beginning of the document, press the Home key twice followed by the up arrow key.

   Press: Home key twice
   Press: up arrow

   The cursor is positioned under the **W** of **When**.

2. To begin the Replace operation, press the Alt-F2 key combination.

   Press: Alt-F2

   The status line displays

   ```
   w/Confirm? No (Yes)
   ```

   By responding to this option, the user indicates if each search item is to be replaced automatically or if the user is to respond to each replacement find.

Type: Y

3. To indicate that each replacement is to be confirmed, type Y.

   The status line displays

   `-> Srch:`

Type: hate

4. Type the word hate as the search text.

Press: F2

5. Press the F2 key to enter the replacement text.

   The status line displays

   `Replace with:`

Type: adore

6. Type the word adore as the replacement text.

Press: F2

7. To begin the search, press the F2 key.

   The cursor moves to the first **hate** that appears in the text. The status line displays

   `Confirm? No (Yes)`

Type: Y

8. To replace the word **hate**, type Y.

   After the word has been replaced, the cursor moves to the next occurrence of **hate**. The status line displays

   `Confirm? No (Yes)`

Type: Y

9. To replace the word **hate**, type Y.

   If the word **hate** had appeared elsewhere in the document, this process would have continued until none were left. As **hate** does not appear elsewhere, the replacement process ends.

Changing Type Styles

The type style of printed materials can be changed by entering the appropriate commands within the text file. WordPerfect supports many print fonts. The styles available are dependent upon the printer, as some styles cannot be produced by certain printers. A daisy wheel printer requires that the print element be changed to access different styles, while a dot matrix or laser printer can produce assorted typefaces and sizes without making physical changes to the printer. On these printers, the print style can be changed from pica to elite to italics from within the word processing program.

Type styles are varied by applying font indicators to blocks of text. Type style commands are entered by pressing the appropriate style key. In WordPerfect, most type fonts and styles are controlled with the Alt-F8 key combination. However, two frequently used type styles are activated with a single keystroke. **Bold** type is turned on and off with the F6 key and underline is turned on and off with the F8 key.

Whenever a type style is entered, the text on the screen is displayed in a different manner. For example, on some screens underlining will appear underlined, on others it will appear in a different shade or color.

To activate a new type style, the cursor is positioned at the location where the text is to be typed and the type style indicator is pressed. For existing text, the text is marked as a block and the key combination associated with the desired font is pressed. To turn off a type style, the key combination used to activate the font is repeated.

To underline the word **adored**, which appears in the second sentence of this exercise paragraph, complete the following steps.

1. Using the arrow keys, position the cursor under the **a** in **adored** in the second sentence.

   Position cursor: at the a in adored

2. To activate the Block command, press the Alt-F4 key combination.

   Press: Alt-F4

   The status line flashes

   ```
   Block on
   ```

3. Using the right arrow key, highlight the word **adored**.

   Highlight: adored

4. To mark the highlighted text for underlining, press the F8 key.

   Press: F8

   Note that the word **adored** is underlined or highlighted. When the paragraph is printed, the word **adored** will be underlined.

Saving a Document

Until a document is saved, any additions or alterations made to it reside only in temporary memory (RAM). If the power fails or the computer is turned off, all additions and changes made to the document are lost. In order to have a permanent copy of a document, the Save command is used to place the document file on disk. Saving a file every 15 minutes can prevent the loss of hours of work should something go wrong.

To save this paragraph to a file on the working data disk, complete the following steps.

Press: F10

1. To activate the Save command, press the F10 key.

   The status line displays

   `Document to be saved:`

2. Specify the name of the file and where it is to be saved. A filename can be eight characters or less in length.

Type: a:exercise

   If a data diskette resides in drive A:, type A:EXERCISE. (Uppercase or lowercase may be used.

   -or-

   If a data diskette does not reside in drive A:, ask your instructor or lab assistant for directions.

Press: <ENTER>

3. To execute the command, press the <ENTER> key.

   The status line indicates the name and location of the saved file **A:\EXERCISE**.

Printing a Document

To obtain a paper copy of the document, the Print command is used. This command is activated by pressing the Shift-F7 key combination to display a list of printing options. To print the Full Document, number 1 is selected from the menu.

Press: Shift-F7

1. To begin the print process, press the Shift-F7 key combination.

   The screen displays

```
Print

     1 - Full Document
     2 - Page
     3 - Document on Disk
     4 - Control Printer
     5 - Multiple Pages
     6 - View Document
     7 - Initialize Printer

Options

     S - Select Printer                       HP LaserJet Series II
     B - Binding Offset                       0"
     N - Number of Copies                     1
     U - Multiple Copies Generated by         WordPerfect
     G - Graphics Quality                     Medium
     T - Text Quality                         High



Selection: 0
```

2. Type 1 to select Full Document. **Type:** 1

After the file has been sent to the printer and while the document is being printed on paper, the exercise text is redisplayed on the monitor and further editing can occur.

If the paper copy reads like that below, it is not a literary masterpiece. However, the exercise has been completed successfully and the basics of word processing have been explored.

```
When I first started to learn about microcomputers, I
did not like them very much.  You might say that I
adored them.  Now that I am learning how to do word
processing on a microcomputer, I know that I adore
them.  I did not understand how they could be useful in
an office and did not want to use one.
```

Your paper copy may not display the same line breaks as those in the above paragraph. Line break locations are dependent upon the printer and type styles in use.

Exiting WordPerfect

This exercise has been completed. To exit the word processing program, complete the following steps.

1. To activate the Exit command, press the F7 key. **Press:** F7

   The status line displays

   `Save document? Yes (No)`

2. As the document has not been changed since it was last saved, type N for no. **Type:** N

   The status line displays:

   `Exit WP? No (Yes)`

3. Type Y to exit WordPerfect. **Type:** Y

   A system prompt (C>, a menu, or something similar) is displayed on the screen.

Conclusion

With the commands demonstrated in this exercise, you are capable of producing a letter or memo free of typing errors. Revisions can be made without retyping the entire document and multiple type styles can be used within the document.

Practice Beginning WordPerfect

1. Practice: Loading WordPerfect
   Entering Text
   Deleting & Inserting Text
   Saving Text
   Exiting WordPerfect

   a. Load WordPerfect as described in the Loading WordPerfect section of the Beginning WordPerfect Exercise.

   b. Type the following paragraph:

      Word processing markedly increases productivity when large numbers of similar documents need to be produced. A letter can be merged with a mailing list yielding a series of personalized letters. This process of joining a form letter with a data base is called mail merge.

   c. Practice moving the cursor around the paragraph by using the arrow, Home, and End keys.

   d. Using the arrow keys, position the cursor under the **m** in the word **markedly**. While holding down the Ctrl key, press the Backspace key. The word **markedly** is deleted. The Ctrl-Backspace key combination deletes words.

   e. Look at the left side of the WordPerfect status line to verify that WordPerfect is in normal mode. If the word **Typeover** is displayed, the Ins key must be pressed to return WordPerfect to normal mode.

   f. Using the arrow keys, move the cursor to the second space immediately after the word **processing** in the first line. Type the word substantially.

   g. Press the F10 key to save the document. If the data diskette resides in drive A:, type a:para1 <ENTER>.

   h. Exit WordPerfect by pressing the F7 key and replying N to the "Save Document?" question.

2. Practice: Loading WordPerfect
   Entering Text
   Copying Text
   Moving Text
   Saving Text
   Exiting WordPerfect

   a. Load WordPerfect as described in the Loading WordPerfect section of the Beginning WordPerfect Exercise.

   b. Type the following paragraph:

      The difference between a typewriter and a word processor becomes apparent with the initial draft of a document. Characters typed on a typewriter appear on paper and characters typed on a computer appear on a monitor. Unlike a traditional typist, the computer user does not listen for a bell to indicate the end of a line because a word processor automatically moves a word down to the next line when the right margin is reached. The Enter key is pressed only to end a paragraph or to finish a short line.

   c. Using the arrow keys, move the cursor to the **C** in the sentence beginning **Characters typed**.

   d. Press the Alt-F4 key combination to begin the copying process.

   e. Using the arrow keys, highlight the entire sentence, including the two spaces after the word **monitor.**

   f. Press the Ctrl-F4 key combination to copy the sentence.

   g. Select the "Block Move" option by typing 1.

   h. Use the arrow keys and space bar to position the cursor two spaces after the end of the last sentence. This is the location for the copied sentence.

i. Press the <ENTER> key to copy the text. The sentence is now replicated at the end of the paragraph.

j. Using the arrow keys, move the cursor to anywhere in the sentence beginning **Unlike a**. This is the sentence that will be moved.

k. Press the Ctrl-F4 key combination to begin the move process. Type a 1 to indicate that the unit to be manipulated is a sentence. Then, type a 1 to perform the move.

l. Determine where the sentence is to be relocated (you decide). Position the cursor at this location using the arrow keys. Press the <ENTER> key to complete the move.

m. Press the F10 key to save the document. If the data diskette resides in drive A:, type a:para2 <ENTER>.

n. Exit WordPerfect by pressing the F7 key and replying N to the "Save Document?" question.

3. Practice: Loading WordPerfect
   Entering Text
   Finding and Replacing Text
   Changing Type Styles
   Printing a Text File
   Saving a Text File
   Exiting WordPerfect

a. Load WordPerfect as described in the Loading WordPerfect section of the Beginning WordPerfect Exercise.

b. Type the following paragraph:

Word processing is used in place of a typewriter and is the most frequently used type of microcomputer application software program. It consists of four basic functions which parallel those used to produce a document with a typewriter — creating, editing, formatting, and printing a document. Letters, memos, reports, briefs, and books are easier to prepare with a word processor than with a typewriter, so someone with limited typing skills can soon become a confident and competent typist when using a word processor.

c. Position the cursor at the beginning of the document by pressing the Home key twice followed by the up arrow key. The cursor appears under the **W** of **Word**.

d. Begin the replace operation by pressing the Alt-F2 key combination.

e. Type Y to indicate that each replace is to be confirmed.

f. Type the word parallel as the search text.

g. Press the F2 key to enter the replacement text.

h. Type the words are similar to as the replacement text.

i. Begin the search by pressing the F2 key. The cursor moves to the word **parallel** in the text.

j. Type Y to replace the highlighted word **parallel**. Since **parallel** appears once, the replace process ends.

k. Use the arrow keys to position the cursor under the **t** in the word **typewriter** in the first line. To underline **typewriter**, press the Alt-F4 key combination.

l. Using the right arrow key, highlight the word **typewriter**. To mark the highlighted text for underlining, press the F8 key. When printed, the word **typewriter** will be underlined.

m. To print the text, press the Shift-F7 key combination. Press the 1 to to select the full document option. The document will be printed.

n. Press the F10 key to save the document. If the data diskette resides in drive A:, type a:para3 <ENTER>.

o. Exit WordPerfect by pressing the F7 key and replying N to the "Save Document?" question.

4. Practice: Loading WordPerfect
Entering Text
Deleting & Inserting Text
Saving Text
Exiting WordPerfect

a. Load WordPerfect as described in the Loading WordPerfect section of the Beginning WordPerfect Exercise.

b. Type the following paragraph:

This lesson describes how to load and use the word processor WordPerfect. The topics covered include: loading the program, creating a document, entering text, modifying text, reformatting text, moving blocks of text, using the find and replace feature, changing type styles, saving a document, printing a document, and exiting the paragraph.

c. Practice moving the cursor around the paragraph by using the arrow, Home, and End keys.

d. Using the arrow keys, position the cursor under the **p** in the word **processor**. While holding down the Ctrl key, press the Backspace key. The word **processor** is deleted. The Ctrl-Backspace key combination deletes words.

e. Look at the left side of the WordPerfect status line to verify that WordPerfect is in normal mode. If the word **Typeover** is displayed, the Ins key must be pressed to return WordPerfect to normal mode.

f. Using the arrow keys, move the cursor to the second space immediately after the word **the** in the second line. Type word processing.

g. Press the F10 key to save the document. If the data diskette resides in drive A:, type a:para4 <ENTER>.

h. Exit WordPerfect by pressing the F7 key and replying N to the "Save Document?" question.

5. Practice: Loading WordPerfect
Entering Text
Copying Text
Moving Text
Saving Text
Exiting WordPerfect

a. Load WordPerfect as described in the Loading WordPerfect section of the Beginning WordPerfect Exercise.

b. Type the following paragraph:

Documents longer than 24 lines are too lengthy to be shown in their entirety on the screen. The up arrow key and down arrow key can be used to bring undisplayed text into view. Moving the cursor up when it is located at the top of the screen displays the preceding line of text on the top of the screen unless the first line of the document is already in view. Likewise, moving the cursor down past the bottom of the screen brings another line of text into view unless the cursor is positioned on the last line of the document.

c. Using the arrow keys, move the cursor to the **M** in the sentence beginning **Moving the cursor**.

d. Press the Alt-F4 key combination to begin the copying process.

e. Using the arrow keys, highlight the entire sentence, including the two spaces after the word **view.**

f. Press the Ctrl-F4 key combination to copy the sentence.

g. Select the "Block Move" option by typing 1.

h. Use the arrow keys to move the cursor to the first space after the end of the last sentence. This is the location for the copied sentence.

i. Press the <ENTER> key to copy the text. The sentence is now replicated at the end of the paragraph.

j. Using the arrow keys, move the cursor to anywhere in the sentence beginning **The up arrow**. This is the sentence that will be moved.

k. Press the Ctrl-F4 key combination to begin the move process. Type a 1 to indicate that the unit to be manipulated is a sentence. Then, type a 1 to perform the move.

l. Determine where the sentence is to be relocated (you decide). Position the cursor at this location using the arrow keys. Press the <ENTER> key to complete the move.

m. Press the F10 key to save the document. If the data diskette resides in drive A:, type a:para5 <ENTER>.

n. Exit WordPerfect by pressing the F7 key and replying N to the "Save Document?" question.

6. Practice: Loading WordPerfect
Entering Text
Finding and Replacing Text
Changing Type Styles
Printing a Text File
Saving a Text File
Exiting WordPerfect

a. Load WordPerfect as described in the Loading WordPerfect section of the Beginning WordPerfect Exercise.

b. Type the following paragraph:

In this example, the block command will not be used to mark a block before selecting the move feature. When a move is selected without first marking a block, the text at the cursor may be chosen as a sentence, paragraph, or page. The cursor is placed anywhere within the unit to be moved and the Ctrl-F4 key combination is pressed. Next, the desired unit is selected. The last step in moving a unit of text is to position the cursor at the location where the moved text is to be placed and to press the <ENTER> key.

c. Position the cursor at the beginning of the document by pressing the Home key twice followed by the up arrow key. The cursor appears under the **I** of **In**.

d. Begin the replace operation by pressing the Alt-F2 key combination.

e. Type Y to indicate that each replace is to be confirmed.

f. Type the word feature as the search text.

g. Press the F2 key to enter the replacement text.

h. Type the word command as the replacement text.

i. Begin the search by pressing the F2 key. The cursor moves to the word **feature** in the text.

j. Type Y to replace the highlighted word **feature**. Since **feature** appears once, the replace process ends.

k. Use the arrow keys to position the cursor under the **a** in the word **anywhere** in the first line. To underline **anywhere**, press the Alt-F4 key combination.

l. Using the right arrow key, highlight the word **anywhere**. To mark the highlighted text for underlining, press the F8 key. When printed, the word **anywhere** will be underlined.

m. To print the text, press the Shift-F7 key combination. Press the 1 to select the full document option. The document will be printed.

n. Press the F10 key to save the document. If the data diskette resides in drive A:, type a:para6 <ENTER>.

o. Exit WordPerfect by pressing the F7 key and replying N to the "Save Document?" question.

7. Practice: Loading WordPerfect
Entering Text
Deleting & Inserting Text
Saving Text
Exiting WordPerfect

a. Load WordPerfect as described in the Loading WordPerfect section of the Beginning WordPerfect Exercise.

b. Type the following paragraph:

Until a document is saved, any additions or alterations made to it reside only in temporary memory (RAM). If the power fails or the computer is turned off, all additions and changes made to the document are lost. In order to have a permanent copy of a document, the Save command is used to place the text file on disk. Saving a file every 15 minutes can prevent the loss of hours of work should something go wrong.

c. Practice moving the cursor around the paragraph by using the arrow, Home, and End keys.

d. Using the arrow keys, position the cursor under the **d** in the word **document**. While holding down the Ctrl key, press the Backspace key. The word **markedly** is deleted. The Ctrl-Backspace key combination deletes words.

e. Look at the left side of the WordPerfect status line to verify that WordPerfect is in normal mode. If the word **Typeover** is displayed, the Ins key must be pressed to return WordPerfect to normal mode.

f. Using the arrow keys, move the cursor to the second space immediately after the first **of** in the last line. Type the word many.

g. Press the F10 key to save the document. If the data diskette resides in drive A:, type a:para7 <ENTER>.

h. Exit WordPerfect by pressing the F7 key and replying N to the "Save Document?" question.

8. Practice: Loading WordPerfect
Entering Text
Copying Text
Moving Text
Saving Text
Exiting WordPerfect

a. Load WordPerfect as described in the Loading WordPerfect section of the Beginning WordPerfect Exercise.

b. Type the following paragraph:

Header and footer lines are entered with the Format command (the Shift-F8 key combination). A header or footer line might include a title or a page number. A header is printed at the top of a page. A footer is printed at the bottom of a page. The header or footer is typed and then a specification is made indicating on which pages the headers/footers are to appear.

c. Using the arrow keys, move the cursor to the **A** in the sentence beginning **A header**.

d. Press the Alt-F4 key combination to begin the copying process.

e. Using the arrow keys, highlight the entire sentence including the two spaces after the word **number.**

f. Press the Ctrl-F4 key combination to copy the sentence.

g. Select the "Block Move" option by typing 1.

h. Use the arrow keys to move the cursor to the first space after the end of the last sentence. This is the location for the copied sentence.

i. Press the <ENTER> key to copy the text. The sentence is now replicated at the end of the paragraph.

j. Using the arrow keys, move the cursor to anywhere in the sentence beginning **A footer**. This is the sentence that will be moved.

k. Press the Ctrl-F4 key combination to begin the move process. Type a 1 to indicate that the unit to be manipulated is a sentence. Then, type a 1 to perform the move.

l. Determine where the sentence is to be relocated (you decide). Position the cursor at this location using the arrow keys. Press the <ENTER> key to complete the move.

m. Press the F10 key to save the document. If the data diskette resides in drive A:, type a:para8 <ENTER>.

n. Exit WordPerfect by pressing the F7 key and replying N to the "Save Document?" question.

9. Practice: Loading WordPerfect
Entering Text
Finding and Replacing Text
Changing Type Styles
Printing a Text File
Saving a Text File
Exiting WordPerfect

a. Load WordPerfect as described in the Loading WordPerfect section of the Beginning WordPerfect Exercise.

b. Type the following paragraph:

Normally page numbering starts with page one and continues in sequence to the end of the document. Sometimes when a document is a part of a series, it must start with a number other than one. The Format Page menu contains a New Page Number command that can be used to change the page number of the current page. This feature can also be used to skip page numbers in the middle of a document.

c. Position the cursor at the beginning of the document by pressing the Home key twice followed by the up arrow key. The cursor appears under the **N** of **Normally**.

d. Begin the Replace operation by pressing the Alt-F2 key combination.

e. Type Y to indicate that each replace is to be confirmed.

f. Type the word starts as the search text.

g. Press the F2 key to enter the replacement text.

h. Type the words begins as the replacement text.

i. Begin the search by pressing the F2 key. The cursor moves to the word starts in the text.

j. Type Y to replace the highlighted word **starts**. Since **starts** appears once, the replace process ends.

k. Use the arrow keys to position the cursor under the **s** in the word **skip** in the first line. To underline **skip**, press the Alt-F4 key combination.

l. Using the right arrow key, highlight the word **skip**. To mark the highlighted text for underlining, press the F8 key. When printed, the word **skip** will be underlined.

m. To print the text, press the Shift-F7 key combination. Press the 1 to to select the full document option. The document will be printed.

n. Press the F10 key to save the document. If the data diskette resides in drive A:, type a:para9 <ENTER>.

o. Exit WordPerfect by pressing the F7 key and replying N to the "Save Document?" question.

10. Practice: Loading WordPerfect
Entering Text
Copying Text
Moving Text
Saving Text
Exiting WordPerfect

a. Load WordPerfect as described in the Loading WordPerfect section of the Beginning WordPerfect Exercise.

b. Type the following paragraph:

A spelling checker and a thesaurus are tools used in conjunction with a word processor facilitating spelling and word selection. Some word processing programs have a built-in spelling checker and thesaurus. Other programs require the use of an independent spelling checker and thesaurus program. An independent spelling checker and thesaurus program is loaded into the computer before any other program is used. Because it is an independent program, it can be used with applications other than word processing. The WordPerfect word processing program used with this text has both.

c. Using the arrow keys, move the cursor to the **O** in the sentence beginning **Other programs**.

d. Press the Alt-F4 key combination to begin the copying process.

e. Using the arrow keys, highlight the entire sentence including the two spaces after the word **program.**

f. Press the Ctrl-F4 key combination to copy the sentence.

g. Select the Block Move option by typing 1.

h. Use the arrow keys to move the cursor to the first space after the end of the last sentence. This is the location for the copied sentence.

i. Press the <ENTER> key to copy the text. The sentence is replicated at the end of the paragraph.

j. Using the arrow keys, move the cursor to anywhere in the sentence beginning **Some word processing**. This is the sentence that will be moved.

k. Press the Ctrl-F4 key combination to begin the move process. Type a 1 to indicate that the unit to be manipulated is a sentence. Then, type a 1 to perform the move.

l. Determine where the sentence is to be relocated (you decide). Position the cursor at this location using the arrow keys. Press the <ENTER> key to complete the move.

m. Press the F10 key to save the document. If the data diskette resides in drive A:, type a:para10 <ENTER>.

n. Exit WordPerfect by pressing the F7 key and replying N to the "Save Document?" question.

1. Using WordPerfect, compose a business letter with the following specifications:
   a. left margin of 1 inch (WordPerfect default setting),
   b. right margin of 1 inch (Word Perfect default setting),
   c. block style; and
   d. print the letter on letterhead stationery.

2. Using the business letter created in project #1, modify the inside address, salutation, and date. Include a personal return address and print the letter on a plain sheet of paper.

3. Create a twenty-question test with WordPerfect. Print the test. Edit the document and scramble the question order by marking and moving blocks of text. Print a second version of the test.

4. Compose and print your resume using WordPerfect.

5. Using a dot matrix or laser printer, create and print an invitation using the enhanced text features of WordPerfect.

6. Describe briefly each of the steps utilized when creating a word-processed document.

7. List five applications for word processing and explain why word processing is a useful tool for increasing productivity in each of the examples.

8. Of all the application software available for microcomputers, word processing software is the most frequently used. Why do you think this is true?

9. Write a holiday letter to your friends and relatives. Have several stock paragraphs (boilerplate) which are common to each letter and include a personalized paragraph to each friend.

10. Write a letter of application for a new job. Include a brief listing of your qualifications. Indent the list 3/4" from the left margin of the letter.

11. Sometimes, when typing the same complex name or term, two letters can be substituted for the name when the document is created. For example, the term **Homo sapiens** might have as its substitute the letters **hs**. Once the document has been completed, a search and replace can be used to change the two characters to the actual term. Experiment with this technique in a short document.

12. Using WordPerfect, write a personal letter to a family member.

13. Using WordPerfect, write a letter to your instructor indicating potential uses of a word processor for your personal and professional activities.

14. Using WordPerfect, write a cover letter to accompany your resume. After printing the letter, change the inside address and job position title and create two new files containing letters to two other potential employers.

15. Key a short poem into a WordPerfect file. Use various type styles to change the visual format of the poem. Print the poem in three different styles.

16. Using WordPerfect, write a short article to be submitted for inclusion in a local newsletter.

17. Use the search and replace function of WordPerfect to change every **I** in the paragraph created in the Beginning WordPerfect Exercise to **we**. Proof the paragraph and revise the text so that the subject **we** has a plural verb.

18. Use the PrtSc key to print three WordPerfect help screens of particular interest to you.

19. Load the EXERCISE file created in the Beginning WordPerfect Exercise. Use the block command to copy text to create a file containing three identical paragraphs. Print this file.

20. Using the file created in project #19 above, use the search and replace function to change the word **hate** in the first paragraph to **despise**. Use the type style function to underline the entire second paragraph. Insert a sentence between the second and third sentence of the third paragraph. Print the new file.

WordPerfect 5.1
Intermediate Exercise

Objectives

Learn how to:

1. Set and use tab stops.

2. Use a hanging indent.

3. Join text files.

4. Be able to

   a. change line spacing,
   b. create header lines,
   c. create footer lines; and
   d. automatically number pages at print time.

5. Paginate a document.

6. Perform global search and replace operations.

7. Perform block delete and undelete operations.

Scope of the Exercise

This lesson describes how to use some of the more advanced features of the WordPerfect word processor. The topics covered include: formatting text, joining files, left margin relocation, multiple line spacing, header lines, footer lines, pagination, global search and replace, deleting a block of text, and undeleting a block of text.

Starting the Lesson

For this lesson, everything to be typed at the keyboard is <u>underlined</u> and also appears in the margin. Text appearing on the computer's screen during the lesson is indicated in `courier type`.

1. Before the WordPerfect program can be used to turn a computer into a word processor, the operating system must be loaded into the computer. If a system prompt (C>, a menu, or something similar) is not displayed on the screen, follow the steps described in the Getting Started Exercise in the DOS module to boot the system.

Boot: the computer

Copy: needed files onto data disk

2. Three data files have been created for use with this exercise. Copy the files PAPER, PARAGRAF, and BIBLIOG from the Exercise Disk provided with this module onto a formatted disk. This disk will be the working data disk.

Insert: data disk in drive A:

3. If you are using a hard drive system and the WordPerfect installation instructions have been followed, WordPerfect resides on the hard drive. Insert the working data diskette containing the above three files into drive A:. Any files created during this lesson also will be saved onto this disk.

-or-

If a computer with a different configuration is being used, ask your instructor or lab assistant for directions specific to your setup.

Loading WordPerfect

The computer must be provided with instructions on how to be a word processor. This is done by loading the WordPerfect program into the computer's temporary memory (RAM). To load WordPerfect and to begin executing the program, complete the following steps.

Type: CD\WP51
Press: <ENTER>
Type: WP

1. If you are using a hard drive, log into the WordPerfect subdirectory by typing CD\WP51 and pressing <ENTER>. Then, type WP. (Uppercase or lowercase may be used.)

-or-

If you are in a lab or network setting, verify the above commands with your instructor or lab assistant.

Press: <ENTER>

2. Execute the above command by pressing the <ENTER> key. The Enter key signals to the computer that the command has been typed and needs to be carried out.

A blank screen is displayed and the status line appears in the lower right corner of the monitor.

Margins and the Format Command

The Format command is used to set all aspects of a document's format. It is used to set the configuration of margins, indentations, and tab stops. The Shift-F8 key combination (while holding down the Shift key, press the F8 key) is used to activate the Format command.

To explore Format command options, the following price list will be created.

```
                      COMPUTER PRICE LIST
                       September 5, 1995
VS-Model 2     640K RAM     two 3.5"     portable   1,299.00
VSC-159-12     768K RAM     two 5.25"    desktop    1,349.00
VSC-286-25     512K RAM     20M hard     desktop    1,899.00
VSF-386-40     1M   RAM     40M hard     desktop    3,399.00

NOTES:         These computers are IBM-compatible and
               include MS-DOS.  All of the listed computers
               have color monitors except the portable.  All
               computers and monitors have a 1-year carry-in
               warranty.
```

Before entering text, the default margin settings will be changed; the left and right margins will be set to one-half inch.

1. Activate the Format command by pressing the Shift-F8 key combination.

   Press: Shift-F8

   The screen displays

```
Format

    1 - Line
            Hyphenation                     Line Spacing
            Justification                   Margins Left/Right
            Line Height                     Tab Set
            Line Numbering                  Widow/Orphan Protection

    2 - Page
            Center Page (top to bottom)     Page Numbering
            Force Odd/Even Page             Paper Size/Type
            Headers and Footers             Suppress
            Margins Top/Bottom

    3 - Document
            Display Pitch                   Redline Method
            Initial Codes/Font              Summary

    4 - Other
            Advance                         Overstrike
            Conditional End of Page         Printer Functions
            Decimal Characters              Underline Spaces/Tabs
            Language                        Border Options

Selection: 0
```

2. To select the Line option, type 1.

   Type: 1

   The screen displays the Line formatting options.

```
Format: Line

     1 - Hyphenation                        No

     2 - Hyphenation Zone - Left            10%
                            Right           4%

     3 - Justification                      Full

     4 - Line Height                        Auto

     5 - Line Numbering                     No

     6 - Line Spacing                       1

     7 - Margins - Left                     0.5"
                   Right                    0.5"

     8 - Tab Set                            Rel: -1", every 0.5"

     9 - Widow/Orphan Protection            No


Selection: 0
```

Type: 7

3. To select Margins, type 7.

   The cursor moves to the left margin, 1" default setting.

Type: .5

4. To indicate a Left margin of one-half inch, type .5.

Press: <ENTER>

5. To enter the setting, press <ENTER>.

   The cursor moves to the right margin, 1" default setting.

Type: .5

6. To indicate a one-half inch Right margin, type .5.

Press: <ENTER>

7. To enter the setting, press <ENTER>.

Press: <ENTER>

8. To return to the Format main menu, press <ENTER>.

Press: <ENTER>

7. To return to the blank document, press <ENTER>.

Centering Text

To center text, the Shift-F6 key combination is pressed and the text is typed. To center the first two lines of the price list, complete the following steps.

Press: Shift -F6

1. To indicate that text is to be centered, press the Shift-F6 key combination.

   The cursor moves to the center of the screen.

Type: COMPUTER PRICE LIST

2. Type COMPUTER PRICE LIST.

   The text is centered on the screen.

Press: <ENTER>

3. To position the cursor on the next line, press <ENTER>.

Press: Shift-F6

4. To indicate that text is to be centered, press the Shift-F6 key combination.

   The cursor moves to the center of the screen.

Type: September 5, 1995

5. Type September 5, 1995.

   The text is centered on the screen.

Press: <ENTER> twice

6. To leave a blank line between the title lines and the body of text, press <ENTER> twice.

Format Command and Tabs

Earlier in this lesson, the Format command was used to set left and right margins. Next, the Format command will be used to set desired tabs. WordPerfect has four types of tab stops. The L (left) tab stop is used to left align text. The R (right) tab stop is used to right align text. The C (center) tab stop centers text on the tab stop. The D (decimal) tab stop is used to align columns of decimal numbers.

To simplify text entry, several tab stops will be used. Indicate the desired tab stops by completing the following steps.

1. To select the Format command, press the Shift-F8 key combination.

   Press: Shift-F8

   The screen displays the main Format menu.

2. To select the Line option, type 1.

   Type: 1

   The screen displays the Line formatting options.

3. To select Tab Set, type 8.

   Type: 8

   The screen displays

```
                    COMPUTER PRICE LIST
                     September 5, 1995







L....L....L....L....L....L....L....L....L....L....L....L....L....L....L....L...
|    ^    |    ^    |    ^    |    ^    |    ^    |    ^    |    ^    |    ^
0"       +1"       +2"       +3"       +4"       +5"       +6"       +7"
Delete EOL (clear tabs); Enter Number (set tab); Del (clear tab);
Type; Left; Center; Right; Decimal; .= Dot Leader; Press Exit when done.
```

   This screen displays the current tab settings. The **L**'s show a left tab stop every one-half inch. One-inch markings are shown by a number and a quotation mark; half inches are shown by the ^(caret) symbol.

4. Before new tab stops can be set, the old tab stops must be cleared.

Press: Ctrl-End

To clear the old tabs, press the Ctrl-End key combination.

The screen displays

```
                        COMPUTER PRICE LIST
                         September 5, 1995









.....................................................................................
|    ^    |    ^    |    ^    |    ^    |    ^    |    ^    |    ^    |    ^
0"        +1"       +2"       +3"       +4"       +5"       +6"       +7"
Delete EOL (clear tabs); Enter Number (set tab); Del (clear tab);
Type; Left; Center; Right; Decimal; .= Dot Leader; Press Exit when done.
```

Three left tab stops and one decimal tab stop need to be set.

Type: 2.6
Press: <ENTER>

5. To set the first tab stop one dot to the right of the 2.5-inch marker, type 2.6 and press <ENTER>.

Type: 4
Press: <ENTER>

6. To set the second tab stop at the 4-inch marker, type 4 and press <ENTER>.

Type: 5.3
Press: <ENTER>

7. To set the third tab stop three dots to the right of the 5-inch marker, type 5.3 and press <ENTER>.

Type: 7.1
Press: <ENTER>

8. To set the final tab stop one dot to the right of the 7-inch marker, type 7.1 and press <ENTER>.

Press: Del key
Type: D

9. To indicate the final tab stop as a decimal tab, press the Del key to remove the L and type D.

   The screen should appear as shown below. If it does not, position the cursor at the improperly placed tab stop, press the Del key to delete it, and enter the tab at its proper location.

Press: Esc key

10. To leave the tab line, press the Esc key.

Press: <ENTER>

11. To exit from the Line menu, press <ENTER>.

Press: <ENTER>

12. To exit from the Format menu and return to the price list, press <ENTER>.

Using Tabs and Indents

The tabs inserted above will be used for text entry in the next part of this exercise. This price list contains a hanging indent. A hanging indent is created by typing the initial text and then pressing the F4 indent key.

To finish entering the price list data, complete the following steps.

1. Type VS-Model 2.
2. Press the Tab key.
3. Type 640K RAM.
4. Press the Tab key.
5. Type two 3.5".
6. Press the Tab key.
7. Type portable.
8. Press the Tab key.
9. Type 1,299.00.

   Notice that until the decimal point is typed, the digits slide to the left as each number is entered. Once the decimal has been typed, entries move to the right.

10. Press <ENTER>.
11. Using the tab key, type the descriptions and prices shown below.

VSC-159-12	768K RAM	two 5.25"	desktop	1,349.00
VSC-286-25	512K RAM	20M hard	desktop	1,899.00
VSF-386-40	1M RAM	40M hard	desktop	3,399.00

12. Press <ENTER> twice to insert a blank line.
13. Type NOTES:.
14. Press the F4 key to begin a hanging indent.

    The cursor jumps to the first tab stop.

Type:	VS-Model 2
Press:	Tab
Type:	640K RAM
Press:	Tab
Type:	two 3.5"
Press:	Tab
Type:	portable
Press:	Tab
Type:	1,299.00
Press:	<ENTER>
Type:	underlined text as shown at left
Press:	<ENTER> twice
Type:	NOTES:
Press:	F4

15. Using the word wrap feature, type the following text.

Type: underlined text as shown at right

These computers are IBM-compatible and include MS-DOS. All of the listed computers have color monitors except the portable. All computers and monitors have a 1-year carry-in warranty.

When entering the above paragraph, do not press the Enter key or the Tab key to line up the text.

When the price list has been typed, save it to disk and clear it from the screen. Using the F10 Save command would save the file; however, it does not clear the document from the screen. The F7 command is used to save a document and clear the screen.

Save the price list and clear the screen by completing the following steps.

Press: F7

1. To activate the Exit command, press the F7 key.

Press: <ENTER>

2. Press <ENTER> to indicate Yes the document is to be saved.

Type: A:PRICES
Press: <ENTER>

3. Indicate the name of the file by typing A:PRICES and pressing <ENTER>.

   The bottom of the screen displays

   ```
   Exit WP? No (Yes)
   ```

Press: <ENTER>

4. To select the No default response to clear the document from the screen and remain in WordPerfect, press <ENTER>.

   No is the default option. The default option, usually the first or highlighted choice, can be selected by pressing the Enter key. The No response also could have been selected by typing the letter N.

Joining Files

Some of the documents created in an office setting contain standard paragraphs, notes, and inside addresses. WordPerfect makes it possible to store standard blocks of text in a file and to read any block into a new document at the proper location.

The first step in the process of joining files is the creation of the text files to be joined. Usually these files are written and typed during normal business operations. As the quantity of standard paragraphs increases, the users' options become more varied. Next, the file that is to contain the final document is created. After this file has been created, separate text files are inserted into it. The cursor is placed at the location of the insertion and the Shift-F10 key combination is pressed. WordPerfect requests the name of the file to be read. Then, the file name is typed. When the Enter key is pressed, the text of the indicated file is displayed at the cursor.

The PAPER, PARAGRAF, and BIBLIOG files are the initial draft of a term paper. Join these files into a single file having the name TERMPAPR by completing the following steps.

1. To Retrieve the PAPER file, the first portion of the term paper, press the Shift-F10 key combination.

   Press: Shift-F10

   The screen displays

   ```
   Document to be retrieved:
   ```

2. Indicate the file to be retrieved by typing A:PAPER and pressing <ENTER>.

   Type: A:PAPER
   Press: <ENTER>

   As the PAPER file is read into the document, two error messages may appear at the bottom of the screen. If these messages appear, your WordPerfect has been set up for a different printer than the one used to create the exercise files. In most cases, these error messages can be ignored.

Next, a new paragraph located in a separate file will be placed into the displayed document. The cursor is positioned at the location of the insertion and the new text is retrieved with the Shift-F10 key combination.

1. Using the arrow keys, position the cursor at the left end of the first line of the second paragraph which begins **What a computer program is determines**.

   Position cursor: at left end of first line, second paragraph

2. To insert the paragraph file, press the Shift-F10 key combination.

   Press: Shift-F10

   The screen displays

   ```
   Document to be retrieved:
   ```

3. To indicate the paragraph file, type A:PARAGRAF and press <ENTER>.

   Type: A:PARAGRAF
   Press: <ENTER>

   A paragraph which begins **In almost no country** is to be inserted into the document.

The final insertion is a bibliography which is placed at the end of the document. The cursor is positioned at the end of the document and the bibliography file is joined to the displayed text.

1. To position the cursor at the end of the file, press the Home key twice followed by the down arrow key.

   Press: Home key twice
   Press: down arrow key

Press: <ENTER>

2. To position the cursor at the left margin below the final line of text, press <ENTER>.

Press: Shift-F10

3. To activate the Retrieve command, press the Shift-F10 key combination.

   The screen displays

   `Document to be retrieved:`

Type: A:BIBLIOG
Press: <ENTER>

4. To indicate the bibliography file, type A:BIBLIOG and press <ENTER>.

   The bibliography is read into the document.

Press: F10

5. To save the document, press the F10 key.

Type: A:TERMPAPR
Press: <ENTER>

6. To name the document, type A:TERMPAPR and press <ENTER>.

   The PAPER, PARAGRAF, and BIBLIOG files have been joined into a single file called TERMPAPR and saved on the working data diskette in drive A:.

The Format Command and Print Options

The Format command is used to alter the printed form of a document. WordPerfect has many print options. Line spacing, page length, page numbers, header lines, and footer lines can be controlled with the Format command. These commands are explained in detail in the WordPerfect manual. A few of the commands are explored in this exercise.

Format commands are placed in the text file by positioning the cursor where the command is to begin. The Format command is activated by pressing the Shift-F8 key combination. The command options are selected from the displayed menus after the Format command has been activated. All text following a Format command is affected. Therefore, if a Format command is to affect the entire document, it is placed on the document's first line. Format commands can be placed throughout a document. Thus, sections of single-, double-, and triple-spaced text can appear within a single document.

Line Spacing

To double space the first paragraph of the paper, complete the following steps.

Press: Home key twice
Press: up arrow key

1. Position the cursor at the top of the document by pressing the Home key twice followed by the up arrow key.

2. Activate the Format command by pressing the Shift-F8 key combination.

   Press: Shift-F8

   The screen displays the Format menu.

3. Select the Line option by typing 1.

   Type: 1

   The screen displays the Line menu.

4. Select Line Spacing by typing 6.

   Type: 6

   The cursor moves to the 1 default line spacing.

5. To set double spacing, type 2 and press <ENTER>.

   Type: 2
   Press: <ENTER>

6. To continue editing the term paper, press <ENTER>twice.

   Press: <ENTER> twice

A quick look at the screen reveals that the entire document has been double spaced. To correct this, reset single spacing at the start of the second paragraph by completing the following steps.

1. Using the down arrow key, position the cursor at the beginning of the second paragraph.

   Position cursor: beginning of second paragraph

2. Activate the Format command by pressing the Shift-F8 key combination.

   Press: Shift-F8

   The screen displays the Format menu.

3. Select the Line option by typing 1.

   Type: 1

   The screen displays the Line menu.

4. Select Line Spacing by typing 6.

   Type: 6

   The cursor moves to the 2 line spacing.

5. To set single spacing, type 1 and press <ENTER>.

   Type: 1
   Press: <ENTER>

6. To continue editing the file, press <ENTER> twice.

   Press: <ENTER> twice

   All of the document except for the first paragraph is displayed in a single-spaced format.

Header and Footer Lines

Header and footer lines are entered with the Format command (the Shift-F8 key combination). A header or footer line might include a title or a page number. A header is printed at the top of a page. A footer is printed at the bottom of a page. The header or footer is typed and then a specification is made indicating on which pages the headers/footers are to appear.

A header or footer can be printed at the left margin, at the right margin, or centered on the line. The header/footer location is indicated with the same Format commands used in text entry. To print at the right margin, a right tab or flush right margin command (the Alt-F6 key combination) is used. To center a header or footer, the Center command (the Shift-F6 key combination) is used. To print at the left margin, the header or footer text is typed and no additional command is specified.

A header is needed in the TERMPAPR file. The header **Software Piracy in Schools** is to be centered at the top of every page.

Press: Home key twice
Press: up arrow key

1. Position the cursor at the top of the document by pressing the Home key twice followed by the up arrow key.

Press: Shift-F8

2. To select the Format command, press the Shift-F8 key combination.

   The screen displays the Format menu.

Type: 2

3. To select the Page option, type 2.

   The screen displays the Page menu.

Type: 3

4. To select the Headers option, type 3.

   The bottom of the screen displays

   `1 Header A; 2 Header B: 0`

Type: 1

5. To select Header A, type 1.

   The bottom of the screen displays

   `1 Discontinue; 2 Every Page; 3 Odd Pages; 4 Even Pages; 5 Edit: 0`

Type: 2

6. To place the header on Every Page, type 2.

   A blank screen is displayed.

Press: Shift-F6

7. To center the header, press the Shift-F6 key combination.

Type: Software Piracy in Schools

8. Type the header Software Piracy in Schools.

Press: F7

9. To exit from the Header option, press the F7 key.

Press: <ENTER> twice

10. To return to editing the file, press the <ENTER> key twice.

Page Numbers

Page numbers can be located at the top or bottom of a page, centered, or aligned with the right or left margins. Page numbers are entered by selecting the Format command (the Shift-F8 key combination) and choosing Page Numbering from the page format menu. The page number can be placed in a header or footer by typing the Ctrl-B key combination in the header or footer line.

To center page numbers on the bottom of every page of the TERMPAPR file, complete the following steps.

1. To select the Format command, press the Shift-F8 key combination. **Press:** Shift-F8

   The screen displays the Format menu.

2. To select the Page option, type 2. **Type:** 2

   The screen displays the Page menu.

3. To select the Page Numbering option, type 6. **Type:** 6

   The screen displays

```
Format: Page Numbering

     1 - New Page Number       1

     2 - Page Number Style     ^B

     3 - Insert Page Number

     4 - Page Number Position No page numbering




Selection: 0
```

4. To select the Page Number Position option, type 4. **Type:** 4

   The screen displays

Format: Page Number Position

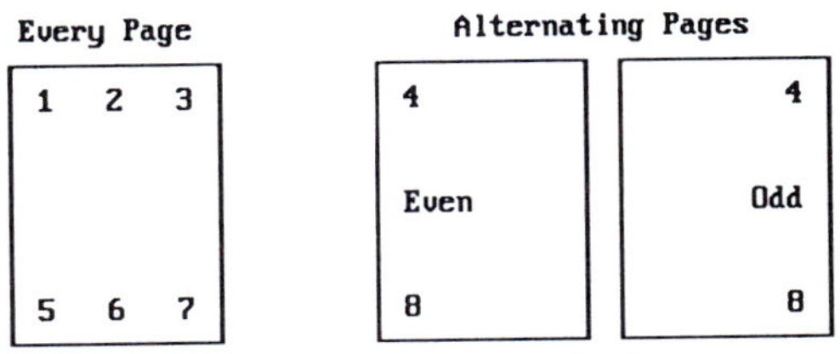

9 - No Page Numbers

Selection: 0

Type: 6

5. To print page numbers centered on the bottom of every page, type 6.

Normally page numbering starts with page one and continues in sequence to the end of the document. Sometimes when a document is a part of a series, it must start with a number other than one. The Format Page menu contains a New Page Number command that can be used to change the page number of the current page. This feature can also be used to skip page numbers in the middle of a document.

To change the starting page number of the TERMPAPR file to 15, complete the following steps.

Type: 1

1. The screen displays the Page Numbering menu.

   To select the New Page Number option, type 1.

   The cursor moves to the right of New Page Number.

Type: 15
Press: <ENTER>

2. To change the beginning page number to 15, type 15 and press <ENTER>.

Press: <ENTER> three times

3. To return to editing the file, press <ENTER> three times.

   The bottom of the screen displays

```
Doc 1  Pg 15  Ln 1.33"  Pos 1"
```

Pagination

In WordPerfect, page breaks are shown by a dashed line on the screen. By examining these lines, improper page breaks can be found and corrected.

There are two types of page breaks. The page breaks automatically created by WordPerfect are soft page breaks. A soft page break is represented by the --- symbols on the screen. Soft page breaks are moved automatically by WordPerfect when a document is changed during the editing process.

A hard page break is created by the user by placing the cursor at the start of a line and pressing the Ctrl-Enter key combination (while holding down the Ctrl key, press the <ENTER> key). A hard page break is represented by the === symbols on the screen. Hard page breaks are inserted to prevent page breaks from occurring in the middle of tables or at other awkward locations and are not moved by WordPerfect when a document is altered. Neither the soft nor the hard page break symbols appear in the printed copy of a file.

The page breaks indicated in the next portion of this exercise will not appear in the same locations on all computer systems because of printer differences. However, the pagination procedures illustrated in this exercise can be applied to all systems. Repeated use of the PgDn key from the beginning of the file places soft page breaks throughout the document and removes any existing soft page breaks from the joined files.

Printer differences and varying default margin settings cause soft page breaks to occur in different locations on varying computer systems. Because of these differences, the default soft page breaks will be accepted for the body of the paper in this exercise. However, a hard page break will be inserted at the top of the bibliography.

To insert three soft page breaks, a hard page break, and a final soft page break into the TERMPAPR file, complete the following steps.

1. Verify that the cursor is positioned at the top of the document.	**Verify:**	cursor location
2. To move to the first page break, press the PgDn key.	**Press:**	PgDn key
3. To position the cursor at the next page break, press the PgDn key.	**Press:**	PgDn key
4. To position the cursor at the next page break, press the PgDn key.	**Press:**	PgDn key
5. To position the cursor at the next page break, press the PgDn key. This page break appears in the center of the bibliography, but the bibliography should begin on a new page.	**Press:**	PgDn key
6. Use the arrow keys to position the cursor at the left of the screen on the title line which reads **Selected Bibliography**.	**Position cursor:**	left of Selected Bibliography
7. To enter a hard page break, press the Ctrl-Enter key combination. The bibliography now begins on a new page.	**Press:**	Ctrl-<ENTER>
8. To move the cursor to the next page break, press the PgDn key.	**Press:**	PgDn key

To view the page breaks on the screen, complete the following steps.

1. Position the cursor at the top of the document by pressing the Home key twice followed by the up arrow key.	**Press:** **Press:**	Home key twice up arrow key
2. Press the grey + key, found on the numeric keypad, several times to scroll through the document to view the file and to locate the soft and hard page breaks.	**Press:**	grey + key

To verify that the headings, page numbering, line spacing, and page breaks have been properly indicated, print the term paper by completing the following steps.

Press: Shift-F7

1. To begin the print process, press the Shift-F7 key combination.

   The screen displays

```
Print

     1 - Full Document
     2 - Page
     3 - Document on Disk
     4 - Control Printer
     5 - Multiple Pages
     6 - View Document
     7 - Initialize Printer

Options

     S - Select Printer                     HP LaserJet Series II
     B - Binding Offset                     0"
     N - Number of Copies                   1
     U - Multiple Copies Generated by       WordPerfect
     G - Graphics Quality                   Medium
     T - Text Quality                       High



Selection: 0
```

Verify: printer option

2. Verify that the printer indicated on the bottom right of the screen is the printer in use.

Type: 1

3. To select the Full Document option, type 1.

When the document has been printed on paper, the text is redisplayed on the monitor and further editing can occur. Look over the printed copy of the term paper to identify any needed corrections.

Global Search and Replace

WordPerfect can search for and replace every occurrence of a misspelled or mistyped word in a document. The Alt-F2 key combination is used to begin the Search and Replace process. Rather than indicating Yes to confirm each replace as demonstrated in the WordPerfect Beginning Exercise, indicate No. Thus, every occurrence of the search text will be replaced without confirmation. Caution must be used when issuing global commands. A search and replace of the word ***ate*** with the word ***eight*** can change h***ate*** to h***eight***. This error could be prevented by entering a space before and after the search text.

Using the TERMPAPR file, replace the word **computer** with **microcomputer** by completing the following steps.

1. Verify that the cursor is positioned at the top of the document.	**Verify:**	cursor at top of document
2. To begin the Search and Replace process, press the Alt-F2 key combination. The bottom of the screen displays `W/Confirm? No (Yes)`	**Press:**	Alt-F2
3. To accept the default No, press <ENTER>. The bottom of the screen displays `-> Srch:`	**Press:**	<ENTER>
4. Type computer as the search word.	**Type:**	computer
5. To continue the process, press the F2 key. The bottom of the screen displays `Replace with:`	**Press:**	F2
6. Type microcomputer as the replace text.	**Type:**	microcomputer
7. To continue the process, press the F2 key.	**Press:**	F2

All occurrences of the word **computer** have been replaced with the word **microcomputer**. A quick examination of the document reveals that using this search and replace procedure has created some problems. The word **micromicrocomputer** has been created in two places. Additional mistakes have occurred in the bibliography. The word **computer** appeared in several of the book and magazine titles and has been changed to **microcomputer**.

The creation of the word **micromicrocomputer** could have been prevented by placing spaces before and after the word **computer** when the search text was indicated. However, this entry would not prevent mistakes from being made in the bibliography. Caution must be used when selecting the No confirmation option in the Search and Replace feature.

Deleting and Undeleting

There are several simple ways to delete text. Pressing the Ctrl-End key combination deletes text from the cursor to the end of the line. Pressing the Ctrl-Backspace key combination deletes one word at the cursor. Pressing the Ctrl-PgDn key combination deletes text from the cursor to the end of the page. A block of marked text is deleted by pressing the Backspace key.

When deleting text with a Ctrl-End, Ctrl-Backspace, or Ctrl-PgDn key combination, or pressing the Backspace key in a marked block, the text is moved into a holding area of the computer's memory and can be retrieved. Since the hold area can contain only one block of text at a time, text is replaced in the hold area when another item is deleted. Text in the hold area can be reinserted into the file by pressing the F1 key.

Delete and restore the last two entries in the bibliography by completing the following steps.

Position cursor: entry 16

1. Using the arrow keys, position the cursor at the beginning of entry 16 in the bibliography.

Press: Ctrl-PgDn

2. To delete entries 16 and 17, press the Ctrl-PgDn key combination.

   The screen displays

   `Delete Remainder of page? No (Yes)`

Type: Y

3. To delete the rest of the page, type Y.

   Entries 16 and 17 have been deleted.

Press: F1

4. To restore the deleted text, press the F1 key.

   The screen displays

   `Undelete: 1 Restore; 2 Previous Deletion: 0`

Type: 1

5. To restore the deleted text, type 1.

Exiting WordPerfect

This lesson has been completed. Exit the word processing program and save the document by completing the following steps.

Press: F7

1. To exit WordPerfect, press the F7 key.

   The bottom of the screen displays

   `Save Document? Yes (No)`

Press: <ENTER>

2. To save the document, press <ENTER>.

   The bottom of the screen displays

   `Document to be saved: A:\TERMPAPR`

3. To save the document with the same file name, press <ENTER>. | **Press:** <ENTER>

   The bottom of the screen displays

   `Replace A:\TERMPAPR?  No  (Yes)`

4. To replace the old version of the document with the revised version, type Y. | **Type:** Y

   The bottom of the screen displays

   `Exit WP? No  (Yes)`

5. To exit from WordPerfect, type Y. | **Type:** Y

   The MS-DOS system prompt (C>, a menu, or something similar) is displayed on the screen.

Conclusion

The commands presented in this exercise simplify text modification and page layout. Productivity will be enhanced when a user knows the commands demonstrated in this lesson.

1. Practice:
   - Loading WordPerfect
   - Using the Format Command
   - Setting Margins
   - Entering Centered Text
   - Setting Tab Stops
   - Setting Decimal Tabs
   - Using Tabs
   - Using Hanging Indents
   - Saving Text
   - Exiting WordPerfect

a. Load WordPerfect as described in the Loading WordPerfect section of the Beginning WordPerfect Exercise .

b. Using the Shift-F8 key combination, activate the Format command.

c. Select the Line option by typing 1.

d. Select the Margins option by typing 7.

e. Indicate a left margin setting of 3/4" by typing .75.

f. Indicate a right margin setting of 3/4" by typing .75.

g. Press <ENTER> to enter each margin setting.

h. Press <ENTER> to return to the Format main menu.

i. Press <ENTER> to return to the blank document.

j. Press the Shift-F6 key combination to activate centering mode. The cursor moves to the center of the screen.

k. Type Travel America Participants and press <ENTER>.

l. Press the Shift-F6 key combination to activate centering mode.

m. Type December 15, 1990 and press <ENTER>.

n. Press <ENTER> twice to create two blank lines in the document.

o. Using the Shift-F8 key combination, activate the Format command.

p. Select the Line option by typing 1.

q. Select the Tab Set option by typing 8. The screen displays the current tab settings.

r. Press the Ctrl-End key combination to clear the old tab stops.

s. Set the first tab stop at .5 inches from the left margin by typing .5 and pressing the <ENTER> key.

t. Set the second tab stop at 3.5 inches from the left margin by typing 3.5 and pressing the <ENTER> key.

u. Set the third tab stop at 5.5 inches from the left margin by typing 5.5 and pressing the <ENTER> key.

v. Set the fourth tab stop at 6.0 inches from the left margin by typing 6.0 and pressing the <ENTER> key.

w. Set the last tab stop at 6.5 inches from the left margin by typing 6.5 and pressing the <ENTER> key.

x. Enter the first line of data with the following key strokes:

   Type John Smith and press the Tab key.

   Type Big Rapids and press the Tab key.

   Type MI and press the Tab key.

   Type 49307 and press <ENTER>.

y. In like manner enter the following names, cities, states, and zip codes:

Dale Hobart	Big Rapids	MI 49307
Sharon Octernaud	Big Rapids	MI 49307
Sid Sytsma	Big Rapids	MI 49307
Bill Doe	Cedar Rapids	NJ 56779
Mary Hart	Hollywood	CA 89999

z. Press the <ENTER> key to create a blank line below the listing of names and addresses.

aa. Type INFO: and press the F4 key to create a hanging indent at the first tab stop.

ab. Type the following paragraph without using the Enter or Tab key.

These names and addresses are a complete listing of all current members in the Ride America Travel Club. Each member has traveled more than 500,000 miles on American public transportation.

ac. Press the F10 key to save the document. If the data diskette resides in drive A:, type A:TABLE1 <ENTER>.

ad. Exit WordPerfect by pressing the F7 key and replying N to the "Save Document?" question.

2. Practice:
   Loading WordPerfect
   Entering Text
   Joining Text Files Residing on Disk
   Changing Line Spacing
   Creating a Header Line in a Document
   Placing Page Numbers in a Document
   Paginating a Document
   Printing a Document
   Saving a Document
   Exiting WordPerfect

a. Load WordPerfect as described in the Loading WordPerfect section of the Beginning WordPerfect Exercise.

b. Create a cover page for a report, containing the following information:

The report title, placed 15 lines from the top of the page and centered by using the Shift-F6 key combination.

Type

Ride America Travel Program
Executive Summary

The date should be placed 25 lines below the report title and should be centered. Type the current date.

c. Save the cover under the filename of COVER by pressing the F10 key. If the data diskette resides in drive A:, type A:COVER <ENTER>.

d. Exit WordPerfect by pressing the F7 key and replying N to the "Save Document?" question.

e. Load WordPerfect as described in the Loading WordPerfect section of the Beginning WordPerfect Exercise.

f. Write a 40-50 line, fictional report on the Ride America Travel Program. Save the report under the filename of BODY by pressing the F10 key. If the data diskette resides in drive A:, type A:BODY <ENTER>.

g. Exit WordPerfect by pressing the F7 key and replying N to the "Save Document?" question.

h. Load WordPerfect as described in the Loading WordPerfect section of the Beginning WordPerfect Exercise.

i. To begin the process of joining the COVER and BODY files created in this practice exercise with the TABLE1 file created in practice exercise #1, press the Shift-F10 key combination. Type A:COVER as the document to be retrieved and press <ENTER>.

j. Using the arrow keys, move the cursor to the end of the COVER file.

k. Press the Shift-F10 key combination and reply to the document retrieval question by typing A:BODY <ENTER>.

l. Press the Shift-F10 key combination and reply to the document retrieval question by typing A:TABLE1 <ENTER>.

m. Change the "report" or BODY section of the text to double spacing by positioning the cursor under the first letter in that section of text by using the arrow keys.

n. Activate the Format command by pressing the Shift-F8 key combination.

o. Select the Line option by typing 1.

p. Select the Line Spacing option by typing 6.

q. Set double spacing by typing 2 and pressing <ENTER>.

r. Press <ENTER> twice to return to the edit mode.

s. Using the arrow keys, move the cursor to the table at the end of the document. Notice that it is double spaced as well.

t. Change the table to single spacing by activating the Format command by pressing the Shift-F8 key combination.

u. Select the Line option by typing 1.

v. Select the Line Spacing option by typing 6.

w. Set single spacing by typing 1 and pressing <ENTER>.

x. Press <ENTER> twice to return to the edit mode.

y. Center the header, **Ride America - Executive Summary**, at the top of each page of the document except for the cover page. Begin this process by positioning the cursor at the beginning of the report section of the document (immediately after the cover) by using the arrow keys.

z. Select the Format command by pressing the Shift-F8 key combination.

aa. Select the Page option by typing 2.

ab. Select the Headers option by typing 3.

ac. Place the header on every page of text after the location of the cursor by typing 2.

ad. To center the header, press the Shift-F6 key combination.

ae. Type Ride America - Executive Summary.

af. Exit from the Header option by pressing the F7 key.

ag. To return to the edit mode, press the <ENTER> key twice.

ah. Place page numbers centered at the bottom of every page except the cover page. The cursor should be located at the beginning of the body of the report, immediately after the cover page. Position the cursor at this location by using the arrow keys.

ai. Activate the Format command by pressing the Shift-F8 key combination.

aj. Select the Page option by typing 2.

ak. Select the Page Numbering option by typing 7.

al. To print numbers centered on the bottom of every page, type 6.

am. To return to the edit mode, press the <ENTER> key twice.

an. This document needs to be paginated. A hard page break should be placed at the beginning of the report section (after the cover) and at the beginning of the table at the end of the document. To begin this process, move the cursor to the first word of the report section by using the arrow keys.

ao. Press the Ctrl-<ENTER> key combination to create a hard page break.

ap. Move the cursor to the beginning of the first line of the table at the end of the document.

aq. Press the Ctrl-<ENTER> key combination to create a hard page break.

ar. Press the F10 key to save the document. If the data diskette resides in drive A:, type A:TRAVEL <ENTER>.

as. Print the document by pressing the Shift-F7 key combination. Type 1 to select the Full Document option. The document should be printed as formatted and paginated.

at. Exit WordPerfect by pressing the F7 key and replying N to the "Save Document?" question.

3. Practice:
   Loading WordPerfect
   Entering Text
   Global Search and Replace
   Deleting and Undeleting
   Exiting WordPerfect

a. Load WordPerfect as described in the Loading WordPerfect section of the Beginning WordPerfect Exercise.

b. Enter the following paragraph:

   WordPerfect can search for and replace every occurrence of a misspelled or mistyped word in a document. The Alt-F2 key combination is used to begin the Search and Replace process. Rather than indicating Yes to confirm each replace as shown in the WordPerfect Beginning Exercise, indicate No. Thus, every occurrence of the search text will be replaced without confirmation. Caution must be used when issuing global commands. A search and replace of the word **ate** with the word **eight** can change h**ate** to h**eight**. This error could be prevented by entering a space before and after the search text.

c. Position the cursor at the beginning of the paragraph by using the arrow keys.

d. Change every occurrence of the word **replace** with the word **change**. Begin this process by pressing the Alt-F2 key combination.

e. Press <ENTER> to accept the default of no confirmation of each replace operation.

f. Type replace as the search word and press the F2 key.

g. Type change as the replace word and press the F2 key. All occurrences of **replace** have been modified to **change**.

h. Practice deleting and undeleting text by placing the cursor under the **T** in **This error** in the last sentence of the paragraph.

i. Press the Ctrl-PgDn key combination to delete everything from the cursor to the end of the page.

j. Restore the deleted text by pressing the F1 key.

k. Complete the restoration process by typing 1.

l. Exit WordPerfect by pressing the F7 key and replying N to the "Save Document?" question.

4. Practice:
    - Loading WordPerfect
    - Using the Format Command
    - Setting Margins
    - Entering Centered Text
    - Setting Tab Stops
    - Setting Decimal Tabs
    - Using Tabs
    - Using Hanging Indents
    - Saving Text
    - Exiting WordPerfect

a. Load WordPerfect as described in the Loading WordPerfect section of the Beginning WordPerfect Exercise .

b. Using the Shift-F8 key combination, activate the Format command.

c. Select the Line option by typing 1.

d. Select the Margins option by typing 7.

e. Indicate a left margin setting of 1/2" by typing .5.

f. Indicate a right margin setting of 1/2" by typing .5.

g. Press <ENTER> to enter each margin setting.

h. Press <ENTER> to return to the Format main menu.

i. Press <ENTER> to return to the blank document.

j. Press the Shift-F6 key combination to activate centering mode. The cursor moves to the center of the screen.

k. Type Statistics Textbooks and press <ENTER>.

l. Press the Shift-F6 key combination to activate centering mode.

m. Type January 25, 1968 and press <ENTER>.

n. Press <ENTER> twice to create two blank lines in the document.

o. Using the Shift-F8 key combination, activate the Format command.

p. Select the Line option by typing 1.

q. Select the Tab Set option by typing 8. The screen displays the current tab settings.

r. Press the Ctrl-End key combination to clear the old tab stops.

s. Set the first tab stop at .5 inches from the left margin by typing .5 and pressing the <ENTER> key.

t. Set the second tab stop at 4.0 inches from the left margin by typing 4.0 and pressing the <ENTER> key.

u. Set the third tab stop at 5.0 inches from the left margin by typing 5.0 and pressing the <ENTER> key.

v. Set the fourth tab stop at 6.0 inches from the left margin by typing 6.0 and pressing the <ENTER> key.

w. Set the last tab stop at 7.0 inches from the left margin by typing 7.0 and pressing the <ENTER> key.

x. Enter the first line of data with the following key strokes: Type Statistics Methods and press the Tab key. Type Excellent and press the Tab key. Type V1 and press the Tab key. Type 1990 and press <ENTER>.

y. In like manner enter the following textbook data:

Analysis, A New Approach	Good	V2	1993
Intro to Inference	Mediocre	V2	1992
Practical Probability	Hard	V1	1995
Lazy Statistics	Easy	V3	1989
Data Analysis	Great	V1	1990

z. Press the <ENTER> key to create a blank line below the listing of textbook data.

aa. Type INFO: and press the F4 key to create a hanging indent at the first tab stop.

ab. Type the following paragraph without using the Enter or Tab key.

These are the titles and ratings of the statistics textbooks selected for final review by the text selection committee.

ac. Press the F10 key to save the document. If the data diskette resides in drive A:, type A:TABLE2 <ENTER>.

ad. Exit WordPerfect by pressing the F7 key and replying N to the "Save Document?" question.

5. Practice:

   Loading WordPerfect
   Entering Text
   Joining Text Files Residing on Disk
   Changing Line Spacing
   Creating a Header Line in a Document
   Placing Page Numbers in a Document
   Paginating a Document
   Printing a Document
   Saving a Document
   Exiting WordPerfect

a. Load WordPerfect as described in the Loading WordPerfect section of the Beginning WordPerfect Exercise.

b. Create a cover page for a report, containing the following information:

   The report title, placed 15 lines from the top of the page and centered by using the Shift-F6 key combination.

   Type

   Final Report
   Statistics Textbook Selection

   The date should be placed 25 lines below the report title and should be centered. Type the current date.

c. Save the cover under the filename of COVER2 by pressing the F10 key. If the data diskette resides in drive A:, type A:COVER2 <ENTER>.

d. Exit WordPerfect by pressing the F7 key and replying N to the "Save Document?" question.

e. Load WordPerfect as described in the Loading WordPerfect section of the Beginning WordPerfect Exercise.

f. Write a 40-50 line, fictional report on the Comparison of Statistics Textbooks. Save the report under the filename of BODY2 by pressing the F10 key. If the data diskette resides in drive A:, type A:BODY2 <ENTER>.

g. Exit WordPerfect by pressing the F7 key and replying N to the "Save Document?" question.

h. Load WordPerfect as described in the Loading WordPerfect section of the Beginning WordPerfect Exercise.

i. To begin the process of joining the COVER2 and BODY2 files created in this practice exercise with the TABLE2 file created in practice exercise #4, press the Shift-F10 key combination. Type A:COVER2 as the document to be retrieved and press <ENTER>.

j. Using the arrow keys, move the cursor to the end of the COVER2 file.

k. Press the Shift-F10 key combination and reply to the document retrieval question by typing A:BODY2 and pressing <ENTER>.

l. Press the Shift-F10 key combination and reply to the document retrieval question by typing A:TABLE2 and pressing <ENTER>.

m. Change the "report" or BODY2 section of the text to double spacing by positioning the cursor under the first letter in that section of text by using the arrow keys.

n. Activate the Format command by pressing the Shift-F8 key combination.

o. Select the Line option by typing 1.

p. Select the Line Spacing option by typing 6.

q. Set double spacing by typing 2 and pressing <ENTER>.

r. Press <ENTER> twice to return to the edit mode.

s. Using the arrow keys, move the cursor to the table at the end of the document. Notice that it is double-spaced as well.

t. Change the table to single spacing by activating the Format command by pressing the Shift-F8 key combination.

u. Select the Line option by typing 1.

v. Select the Line Spacing option by typing 6.

w. Set single spacing by typing 1 and pressing <ENTER>.

x. Press <ENTER> twice to return to the edit mode.

y. Center the header, **Textbook Selection**, centered at the top of each page of the document except for the cover page. Begin this process by positioning the cursor at the beginning of the report section of the document (immediately after the cover) by using the arrow keys.

z. Select the Format command by pressing the Shift-F8 key combination.

aa. Select the Page option by typing 2.

ab. Select the Headers option by typing 3.

ac. Place the header on every page of text after the location of the cursor by typing 2.

ad. To center the header, press the Shift-F6 key combination.

ae. Type Textbook Selection.

af. Exit from the Header option by pressing the F7 key.

ag. To return to the edit mode, press the <ENTER> key twice.

ah. Place page numbers centered at the bottom of every page except the cover page. The cursor should be located at the beginning of the body of the report, immediately after the cover page. Position the cursor at this location by using the arrow keys.

ai. Activate the Format command by pressing the Shift-F8 key combination.

aj. Select the Page option by typing 2.

ak. Select the Page Numbering option by typing 7.

al. To print numbers centered on the bottom of every page, type 6.

am.To return to the edit mode, press the <ENTER> key twice.

an.This document needs to be paginated. A hard page break should be placed at the beginning of the report section (after the cover) and at the beginning of the table at the end of the document. To begin this process, move the cursor to the first word of the report section by using the arrow keys.

ao. Press the Ctrl-<ENTER> key combination to create a hard page break.

ap. Move the cursor to the beginning of the first line of the table at the end of the document.

aq. Press the Ctrl-<ENTER> key combination to create a hard page break.

ar. Press the F10 key to save the document. If the data diskette resides in drive A:, type A:TEXTBOOK <ENTER>.

as. Print the document by pressing the Shift-F7 key combination. Type 1 to select the Full Document option. The document should be printed as formatted and paginated.

at. Exit WordPerfect by pressing the F7 key and replying N to the "Save Document?" question.

6. Practice:
   Loading WordPerfect
   Entering Text
   Global Search and Replace
   Deleting and Undeleting
   Exiting WordPerfect

a. Load WordPerfect as described in the Loading WordPerfect section of the Beginning WordPerfect Exercise.

b. Enter the following paragraph:

   Programs are sets of instructions enabling the computer to become a productive tool. These programs are known as software. Software programs range from word processors to games and from operating systems to artificial intelligence languages. Microcomputer software can be categorized into three functional types: operating system software, application software, and language software. Software is also categorized according to licensing requirements. These classifications are proprietary, shareware/freeware, and public domain.

c. Position the cursor at the beginning of the paragraph by using the arrow keys.

d. Change every occurrence of the word **programs** to the words **computer programs**. Begin this process by pressing the Alt-F2 key combination.

e. Press <ENTER> to accept the default of no confirmation of each Replace operation.

f. Type replace as the search word and press the F2 key.

g. Type change as the replace word and press the F2 key. All occurrences of **programs** have been modified to **computer programs**.

h. Practice deleting and undeleting text by placing the cursor under the **T** in **These classifications** in the last sentence of the paragraph.

i. Press the Ctrl-PgDn key combination to delete everything from the cursor to the end of the page.

j. Restore the deleted text by pressing the F1 key.

k. Complete the restoration process by typing 1.

l. Exit WordPerfect by pressing the F7 key and replying N to the "Save Document?" question.

7. Practice:
   Loading WordPerfect
   Using the Format Command
   Setting Margins
   Entering Centered Text
   Setting Tab Stops
   Setting Decimal Tabs
   Using Tabs
   Using Hanging Indents
   Saving Text
   Exiting WordPerfect

a. Load WordPerfect as described in the Loading WordPerfect section of the Beginning WordPerfect Exercise .

b. Using the Shift-F8 key combination, activate the Format command.

c. Select the Line option by typing 1.

d. Select the Margins option by typing 7.

e. Indicate a left margin setting of 1.0" by typing 1.0.

f. Indicate a right margin setting of 1.0" by typing 1.0.

g. Press <ENTER> to enter each margin setting.

h. Press <ENTER> to return to the Format main menu.

i. Press <ENTER> to return to the blank document.

j. Press the Shift-F6 key combination to activate centering mode. The cursor moves to the center of the screen.

k. Type Rating College Instructors and press <ENTER>.

l. Press the Shift-F6 key combination to activate centering mode.

m. Type June 21, 1991 <ENTER>.

n. Press <ENTER> twice to create two blank lines in the document.

o. Using the Shift-F8 key combination, activate the Format command.

p. Select the Line option by typing 1.

q. Select the Tab Set option by typing 8. The screen displays the current tab settings.

r. Press the Ctrl-End key combination to clear the old tab stops.

s. Set the first tab stop at .5 inches from the left margin by typing .5 and pressing the <ENTER> key.

t. Set the second tab stop at 2.5 inches from the left margin by typing 2.5 and pressing the <ENTER> key.

u. Set the third tab stop at 5.0 inches from the left margin by typing 5.0 and pressing the <ENTER> key.

v. Set the fourth tab stop at 5.5 inches from the left margin by typing 5.5 and pressing the <ENTER> key.

w. Set the last tab stop at 6.0 inches from the left margin by typing 6.0 and pressing the <ENTER> key.

x. Enter the first line of data with the following key strokes:

Type John Doe and press the Tab key.

Type Computer Sci and press the Tab key.

Type Asst and press the Tab key.

Type 1989 and press <ENTER>.

y. In like manner enter the following names, departments, ranks, and dates:

```
Fred Smith      Statistics   Assoc   1990
Mary Thistle    History      Instr   1989
James Bozo      Humanities   Prof    1992
Sue Sampson     English      Instr   1996
Mary Hart       Math         Prof    1993
```

z. Press the <ENTER> key to create a blank line below the listing of names and other information.

aa. Type INFO: and press the F4 key to create a hanging indent at the first tab stop.

ab. Type the following paragraph without using the Enter or Tab key.

These names and related information include the faculty recommended for promotions immediately upon reaching the minimum date listed for promotion eligibility.

ac. Press the F10 key to save the document. If the data diskette resides in drive A:, type A:TABLE3 <ENTER>.

ad. Exit WordPerfect by pressing the F7 key and replying N to the "Save Document?" question.

8. Practice:

    Loading WordPerfect
    Entering Text
    Joining Text Files Residing on Disk
    Changing Line Spacing
    Creating a Header Line in a Document
    Placing Page Numbers in a Document
    Paginating a Document
    Printing a Document
    Saving a Document
    Exiting WordPerfect

    a. Load WordPerfect as described in the Loading WordPerfect section of the Beginning WordPerfect Exercise.

    b. Create a cover page for a report, containing the following information:

       The report title, placed 15 lines from the top of the page and centered by using the Shift-F6 key combination.

       Type

       Promotion Recommendations
       University College System

       The date should be placed 25 lines below the report title and should be centered. Type the current date.

    c. Save the cover under the filename of COVER3 by pressing the F10 key. If the data diskette resides in drive A:, type A:COVER3 <ENTER>.

    d. Exit WordPerfect by pressing the F7 key and replying N to the "Save Document?" question.

    e. Load WordPerfect as described in the Loading WordPerfect section of the Beginning WordPerfect Exercise.

    f. Write a 40-50 line, fictional report on the Descriptions of Faculty Teaching Performance. Save the report under the filename of BODY3 by pressing the F10 key. If the data diskette resides in drive A:, type A:BODY3 <ENTER>.

    g. Exit WordPerfect by pressing the F7 key and replying N to the "Save Document?" question.

    h. Load WordPerfect as described in the Loading WordPerfect section of the Beginning WordPerfect Exercise.

    i. To begin the process of joining the COVER3 and BODY3 files created in this practice exercise with the TABLE3 file created in practice exercise #7, press the Shift-F10 key combination. Type A:COVER3 as the document to be retrieved and press <ENTER>.

    j. Using the arrow keys, move the cursor to the end of the COVER file.

    k. Press the Shift-F10 key combination and reply to the document retrieval question by typing A:BODY3 and pressing <ENTER>.

    l. Press the Shift-F10 key combination and reply to the document retrieval question by typing A:TABLE3 <ENTER>.

    m. Change the "report" or BODY3 section of the text to double spacing by positioning the cursor under the first letter in that section of text by using the arrow keys.

    n. Activate the Format command by pressing the Shift-F8 key combination.

    o. Select the Line option by typing 1.

    p. Select the Line Spacing option by typing 6.

    q. Set double spacing by typing 2 and pressing <ENTER>.

    r. Press <ENTER> twice to return to the edit mode.

    s. Using the arrow keys, move the cursor to the table at the end of the document. Notice that it is double-spaced as well.

t. Change the table to single spacing by activating the Format command by pressing the Shift-F8 key combination.

u. Select the Line option by typing 1.

v. Select the Line Spacing option by typing 6.

w. Set single spacing by typing 1 and pressing <ENTER>.

x. Press <ENTER> twice to return to the edit mode.

y. Center the header, **Promotion Recommendations**, at the top of each page of the document except for the cover page. Begin this process by positioning the cursor at the beginning of the report section of the document (immediately after the cover) by using the arrow keys.

z. Select the Format command by pressing the Shift-F8 key combination.

aa. Select the Page option by typing 2.

ab. Select the Headers option by typing 3.

ac. Place the header on every page of text after the location of the cursor by typing 2.

ad. To center the header, press the Shift-F6 key combination.

ae. Type Promotion Recommendations.

af. Exit from the Header option by pressing the F7 key.

ag. To return to the edit mode, press the <ENTER> key twice.

ah. Place page numbers centered at the bottom of every page except the cover page. The cursor should be located at the beginning of the body of the report, immediately after the cover page. Position the cursor at this location by using the arrow keys.

ai. Activate the Format command by pressing the Shift-F8 key combination.

aj. Select the Page option by typing 2.

ak. Select the Page Numbering option by typing 7.

al. To print numbers centered at the bottom of every page, type 6.

am. To return to the edit mode, press the <ENTER> key twice.

an. This document needs to be paginated. A hard page break should be placed at the beginning of the report section (after the cover) and at the beginning of the table at the end of the document. To begin this process, move the cursor to the first word of the report section by using the arrow keys.

ao. Press the Ctrl-<ENTER> key combination to create a hard page break.

ap. Move the cursor to the beginning of the first line of the table at the end of the document.

aq. Press the Ctrl-<ENTER> key combination to create a hard page break.

ar. Press the F10 key to save the document. If the data diskette resides in drive A:, type A:PROMO <ENTER>.

as. Print the document by pressing the Shift-F7 key combination. Type 1 to select the Full Document option. The document should be printed as formatted and paginated.

at. Exit WordPerfect by pressing the F7 key and replying N to the "Save Document?" question.

9. Practice: Loading WordPerfect
Entering Text
Global Search and Replace
Deleting and Undeleting
Exiting WordPerfect

a. Load WordPerfect as described in the Loading WordPerfect section of the Beginning WordPerfect Exercise.

b. Enter the following paragraph:

The operating system used on MS-DOS-compatible computers consists of three parts. The first part is built into the control portion of the computer's ROM. The second part is transferred from disk into the computer's RAM when the system is turned on and remains in the computer's RAM until the power is turned off. This transfer process is known as booting the system. The third part of the operating system is placed in an infrequently used section of RAM and stays there until another program requires the space. Should this third portion of the operating system be replaced by another program, the second part of the operating system will try to find the third part on disk. If the third part is not found, the user receives a message to insert a diskette containing the operating system file called COMMAND.COM. The term file refers to programs or information stored by name on a computer disk.

c. Position the cursor at the beginning of the paragraph by using the arrow keys.

d. Change every occurrence of the word **message** to the word **warning**. Begin this process by pressing the Alt-F2 key combination.

e. Press <ENTER> to accept the default of no confirmation of each Replace operation.

f. Type message as the search word and press the F2 key.

g. Type warning as the replace word and press the F2 key. All occurrences of **message** have been modified to **warning**.

h. Practice deleting and undeleting text by placing the cursor under the **f** in **file** in the last sentence of the paragraph.

i. Press the Ctrl-PgDn key combination to delete everything from the cursor to the end of the page.

j. Restore the deleted text by pressing the F1 key.

k. Complete the restoration process by typing 1.

l. Exit WordPerfect by pressing the F7 key and replying N to the "Save Document?" question.

10. Practice:
Loading WordPerfect
Entering Text
Copying Text
Moving Text
Saving Text
Exiting WordPerfect

a. Load WordPerfect as described in the Loading WordPerfect section of the Beginning WordPerfect Exercise.

b. Type the following paragraph:

A spelling checker and a thesaurus are tools used in conjunction with a word processor, facilitating spelling and word selection. Some word processing programs have a built-in spelling checker and thesaurus. Other programs require the use of an independent spelling checker and thesaurus program. An independent spelling checker and thesaurus program is loaded into the computer before any other program is used. Because it is an independent program, it can be used with applications other than word processing. The WordPerfect word processing program used with this text has both.

c. Using the arrow keys, move the cursor to the **O** in the sentence beginning **Other programs**.

d. Press the Alt-F4 key combination to begin the copying process.

e. Using the arrow keys, highlight the entire sentence including the two spaces after the word **program.**

f. Press the Ctrl-F4 key combination to copy the sentence.

g. Select the Block Move option by typing 1. Then type 2 to copy the marked text.

h. Use the arrow keys to move the cursor to the first space after the end of the last sentence. This is the location for the copied sentence.

i. Press the <ENTER> key to copy the text. The sentence is replicated at the end of the paragraph.

j. Using the arrow keys, move the cursor to anywhere in the sentence beginning **Some word processing**. This is the sentence that will be moved.

k. Press the Ctrl-F4 key combination to begin the move process. Type a 1 to indicate that the unit to be manipulated is a sentence. Then, type a 1 to perform the move.

l. Determine where the sentence is to be relocated (you decide). Position the cursor at this location using the arrow keys. Press the <ENTER> key to complete the move.

m. Press the F10 key to save the document. If the data diskette resides in drive A:, type a:para10 <ENTER>.

n. Exit WordPerfect by pressing the F7 key and replying N to the "Save Document?" question.

1. Create three separate document files in WordPerfect containing data to be used as text input files. A text file will be created for each of the following specifications:

   a. a return address, saved under the file name **RETURN**,
   b. a short paragraph asking that the enclosed form be completed and returned within two weeks, saved under the file name **STDPGRF**; and
   c. a closing paragraph, complete with closing and space for signature, saved under the file name of **CLOSING**.

2. Use the three text files created in practice exercise #1. Write and print five letters to five different individuals with the following specifications:

   a. the return address from the **RETURN** file,
   b. an inside address specific to the individual,
   c. the standard paragraph from the **STDPGRF** file,
   d. a second paragraph personalized to the individual; and
   e. the standard closing paragraph from the **CLOSING** file.

3. Using WordPerfect, create a ten-page research paper. Incorporate the following features into the file:

   a. automatic page numbering,
   b. double spacing except for the bibliography,
   c. a header line,
   d. a title page; and
   e. a bibliography.

   Paginate the document appropriately, with hard page breaks at the beginning of the text material (after the title page) and at the beginning of the bibliography. Save the document on disk.

4. Create a memo template to include the following information:

   a. the name of your business/institution centered as a header at the top of a page; and
   b. four lines containing the entries To:, From:, Subject:, and Date:.

   Print a blank memo page. Then, bring up the memo template and write a short memo to your boss.

5. Create a five-column chart displaying the name, city, state, age, and sex of ten people. Use tab stops to align the columns.

6. Create a single-spaced, two-page document with a header on each page. Paginate the document. Print the page with page numbers centered at the bottom of each page.

7. Use the document created in practice exercise #3. Change the line spacing to double space, repaginate the document, and reprint the complete document with page numbers at the bottom right of each page.

8. Retrieve the PRICES file created in the WordPerfect Intermediate Exercise. Save this file under a new name and call it PRICES2. Change the left and right margin settings to 1.5".

9. Use WordPerfect to create a notice to be displayed on an organization's bulletin board announcing the annual membership picnic. Center lines of text and use various type styles to enhance the appearance and legibility of the notice.

10. Retrieve the PRICES file created in the WordPerfect Intermediate Exercise. Save this file under a new name and call it PRICES3. Prices for each of the models have been reduced by $100.00. Edit the PRICES3 file to indicate this price change.

11. Copy the BIBLIOG file from the Exercise Disk onto your working data disk. Join the PRICES file created in the WordPerfect Intermediate Exercise and the BIBLIOG file and save these joined files with the filename RESOURCES. Paginate the document so that the bibliography begins at the top of a page.

12. Copy the PAPER file from the Exercise Disk onto your working data disk. Retrieve this file and save it under a new filename called PAPER2. Use the Format command to print this paper at 4 lines per inch. Be sure to paginate the document to insert hard page breaks where needed.

13. Retrieve the TERMPAPR file created in the WordPerfect Intermediate Exercise. Save this file under a new name and call it TERMPAP2. Include a header centered at the top of every page which indicates that this is DRAFT #1, followed by the current date. Number alternating pages at the bottom of every page with the first page being number 3.

14. Copy the PAPER file from the Exercise Disk onto your working data disk. Retrieve this file and save it under a new filename called PAPER3. Use the Search and Replace function to change the word **law** to **legislation**.

15. Using the tabs in WordPerfect, create in a columnar format a listing of twenty classes, which includes the course title, the number of hours the class meets weekly, the instructor's last name, and the room location.

16. Using indents and tabs in WordPerfect, create a file containing one of your favorite recipes. The ingredients are to be listed in two columns at the top of the page below a centered title. Directions are to follow the ingredients in a single-column format across the width of the page. A left margin of 2" will permit hole punching of the printed document. The right margin is to be 1.5". Print the document twice using two different type styles.

17. Retrieve the recipe file created in practice exercise #16 above. Edit the recipe to serve twice as many people. Save the file under a new filename and print the document.

18. Retrieve the file created in practice exercise #16 above. Print the recipe double spaced.

19. Retrieve the file created in practice exercise #16 above. Print the recipe at five lines per inch.

20. Copy the BIBLIOG file from the Exercise Disk onto your working data disk. Retrieve this file and save it under a new filename called BIBORDER. Use the WordPerfect Move command to change this listing from alphabetical order to chronological order.

21. Use WordPerfect to create and print an outline of the word processing features introduced in the WordPerfect Intermediate Exercise.

22. Use WordPerfect to create and print paper copies that will be used to make transparencies for lecture support when presenting the features outlined in practice exercise #21 above.

WordPerfect 5.1
Advanced Exercise

Objectives

Learn how to:

1. Place several font styles within a document.
2. Display a page on the screen in the same format as the printer would print it.
3. Create a master document with subdocuments.
4. Print a master document.
5. Create footnotes.
6. Create an index.
7. Display and modify embedded WordPerfect formatting codes.
8. Use the Window command to display two files on the screen.

Scope of the Exercise

This lesson describes how to use some of the more advanced features of the WordPerfect word processor. The topics covered include: placing several font styles within a document; creating a master document with subdocuments; creating footnotes, tables of contents and indexes; revealing and manipulating format codes; and using windows to display two files on the screen.

Starting the Lesson

For this lesson, everything to be typed at the keyboard is underlined and also appears in the margin. Text appearing on the computer's screen during the lesson is indicated in `courier type`.

1. Before the WordPerfect program can be used to turn a computer into a word processor, the operating system must be loaded into the computer. If a system prompt (C>, a menu, or something similar) is not present on the screen, follow the steps described in the Getting Started Exercise in the DOS module to boot the system.

Boot: the computer

Copy: needed files onto data disk

2. Four data files are used with this exercise. The files PRICES, PAPER, PARAGRAF, and BIBLIOG used or created in the WordPerfect Intermediate Exercise are needed for this lesson. These files must reside on the working data disk.

Insert: data disk in drive A:

3. If you are using a hard drive system and the WordPerfect installation instructions have been followed, WordPerfect resides on the hard drive. Insert a working data diskette containing the above four files into drive A:. Any files created during this lesson also will be saved onto this disk.

-or-

If a computer with a different configuration is being used, ask your instructor or lab assistant for directions specific to your setup.

Loading WordPerfect

The computer must be provided with instructions on how to be a word processor. This is done by loading the WordPerfect program into the computer's temporary memory (RAM). To load WordPerfect and to begin executing the program, complete the following steps.

Type: CD\WP51
Press: <ENTER>
Type: WP

1. If you are using a hard drive system, log into the WordPerfect subdirectory by typing CD\WP51 and pressing <ENTER>. Then, type WP. (Uppercase or lowercase may be used.)

-or-

If you are in a lab or network setting, verify the above commands with your instructor or lab assistant.

Press: <ENTER>

2. Execute the above command by pressing the <ENTER> key. The Enter key signals to the computer that the command has been typed and needs to be carried out.

Font Types Revisited

In the WordPerfect Intermediate Exercise, the bold and underline font commands were explored. This portion of the lesson investigates the extensive font selection and adjustment commands in WordPerfect. The help screens under each font heading describe the options available for use based upon the printer available.

In order to examine these font commands, load the PRICES file created in the WordPerfect Intermediate Exercise into WordPerfect by completing the following steps.

1. To activate the File Retrieve command, press the Shift-F10 key combination.

   Press: Shift-F10

   The screen displays

   `Document to be retrieved:`

2. To indicate the file to be retrieved, type A:PRICES and press <ENTER>.

   Type: A:PRICES
   Press: <ENTER>

   The file containing a computer price list is loaded into WordPerfect.

The Font command can be used to create superscripts and subscripts and to vary font styles and sizes. The font choices displayed will vary depending upon the printer in use. The following examples were created on a HP LaserJet Series II printer using no soft fonts or cartridge fonts.

To explore the Font command, complete the following steps.

1. Verify that the cursor is positioned at the top of the document. (Press the Home key twice followed by the up arrow key.)

   Verify: cursor at top
   Press: Home key twice
   Press: up arrow key

2. To view the document as it would appear on the printed page, press the Shift-F7 key combination followed by 6.

   Press: Shift-F7
   Type: 6

   The entire page is displayed on the screen.

3. To return to the editing mode, press the F7 key.

   Press: F7

4. To change the size of the current font, activate the Font command by pressing the Ctrl-F8 key combination.

   Press: Ctrl-F8

   The bottom of the screen displays.

   `1 Size; 2 Appearance; 3 Normal; 4 Base Font; 5 Print Color: 0`

   Each of the above options is used to control different font features. An option can be selected by typing the corresponding number and pressing <ENTER>. The Size option sets the basic font size. The Appearance option sets features such as bold, italics, and underline. The Normal option sets the font to the normal default type style. The Base Font option selects the normal default font style. The Print Color option sets colors on printers capable of color printing.

   Selecting Size displays the following option list at the bottom of the screen.

   `1 Suprscpt; 2 Subscpt; 3 Fine; 4 Small; 5 Large; 6 Vry Large; 7 Ext Large: 0`

Most printers will not support all of the above features. Many printers will support superscript and subscript fonts, but experimentation is required to determine the result of selecting a particular option with a given printer.

Selecting Appearance displays the following menu.

```
1 Bold 2 Undrln 3 Dbl Und 4 Italc 5 Outln 6 Shadw 7 Sm Cap 8 Redln 9 Stkout: 0
```

Selecting any of the above options turns that particular option on or off. Most printers will not support all of the above features, but all printers should be able to print bold and underlined characters.

Selecting Normal sets the font to the normal default typeface with no enhancements and returns the cursor to the document. The normal typeface varies with each printer and is controlled with the Base Font selection.

```
Base Font

* Courier 10cpi
  Courier 10cpi Bold
  Line Draw 10cpi (Full)
  Line Printer 16.67cpi
```

Selecting Base Font displays the typeface style and size options available for the current printer. For the Hewlett Packard LaserJet Series II printer, the screen displays the options at the left.

Selecting any of the options changes the normal default font. The font indicated with an asterisk (*) is the current base font.

Selecting Print Color displays the following menu.

```
Print Color

                         Primary Color Mixture
                        Red      Green      Blue

  1 - Black              0%        0%         0%
  2 - White            100%      100%       100%
  3 - Red               67%        0%         0%
  4 - Green              0%       67%         0%
  5 - Blue               0%        0%        67%
  6 - Yellow            67%       67%         0%
  7 - Magenta           67%        0%        67%
  8 - Cyan               0%       67%        67%
  9 - Orange            67%       25%         0%
  A - Gray              50%       50%        50%
  N - Brown             67%       33%         0%
  O - Other

  Current Color          0%        0%         0%


Selection: 0
```

These color features can be used only with color printers. The Other option is used to create customized colors.

5. To select the Base Font option, type 4. — **Type:** 4

A screen similar to that below is displayed.

```
Base Font

* Courier 10cpi
  Courier 10cpi Bold
  Line Draw 10cpi (Full)
  Line Printer 16.67cpi




1 Select; N Name search: 1
```

All of the options may not be displayed on the screen. Pressing the down arrow key may bring additional font choices into view.

6. Use the arrow keys to select a font smaller than the current font. In this example, **`Line Printer 16.67cpi`** could be selected. You may have the option of choosing either Pica (10 **c**haracters **p**er **i**nch) or Elite (12 cpi). Elite is a smaller type than Pica. — **Press:** arrow keys

7. To activate the font, press <ENTER>. — **Press:** <ENTER>

   The document automatically reformats for the new typeface. However, no visible change appears on the screen.

8. To view the document as it would appear on the printed page, press the Shift-F7 key combination followed by 6. — **Press:** Shift-F7 **Type:** 6

   The reformatted price list is displayed on the screen.

9. To return to the editing mode, press the F7 key. — **Press:** F7

10. To print the price list in the new type size, press the Shift-F7 key combination followed by 1. — **Press:** Shift-F7 **Type:** 1

    The reformatted price list is printed in a smaller typeface than that used in the original document.

Text Format Codes

Many complex formatting tasks are performed by WordPerfect behind the scenes. In this portion of the exercise, some of the formatting codes embedded in WordPerfect documents will be examined.

To examine the embedded codes in the PRICES file, complete the following steps.

1. Verify that the cursor is positioned at the top of the document. (Press the Home key twice followed by the up arrow key.) — **Verify:** cursor at top of document

Press: Alt-F3

2. To display the hidden codes, press the <u>Alt-F3</u> key combination.

   The display is similar to that shown below

```
                              COMPUTER PRICE LIST
                               September 5, 1995

VS-Model 2                 640K RAM      two 3.5"     portable      1,299.00
VSC-159-12                 640K RAM      two 5.25"    desktop       1,349.00
VSC-286-25                 512K RAM      20M hard     desktop       1,899.00
VSF-386-40                 1M RAM        40M hard     desktop       3,399.00

NOTES:                     These computers are IBM-comptible and include MS-DOS.
                           have color monitors except the portable.  All computer
                           carry-in warranty.
A:\PRICES                                                Doc 1 Pg 1 Ln 1" Pos 0.5"
{    ▲    ▲    ▲    ▲    ▲    ▲    ▲    ▲    ▲    ▲    ▲    ▲    ▲    ▲    }
[L/R Mar:0.5",0.5"][Font:Line Printer 16.67cpi][Center]COMPUTER PRICE LIST[HRt]
[Center]September 5, 1995[HRt]
[HRt]
[Tab Set:Rel: -0.5",+2.6",+4",+5.3",+7.1"]VS[-]Model 2[Tab]640K RAM[Tab]two 3.5"
[Tab]portable[Dec Tab]1,299.00[HRt]
VSC[-]159[-]12[Tab]640K RAM[Tab]two 5.25"[Tab]desktop[Dec Tab]1,349.00[HRt]
VSC[-]286[-]25[Tab]512K RAM[Tab]20M hard[Tab]desktop[Dec Tab]1,899.00[HRt]
VSF[-]386[-]40[Tab]1M RAM[Tab]40M hard[Tab]desktop[Dec Tab]3,399.00[HRt]
[HRt]
NOTES:[→Indent]These computers are IBM[-]comptible and include MS[-]DOS.  All of

Press Reveal Codes to restore screen
```

The top half of the screen displays the document in the normal mode. The bottom half of the screen below the triangles displays the text and the formatting codes embedded in it by WordPerfect.

The embedded codes are enclosed in square brackets. The first entry on the screen for the PRICES file created in the WordPerfect Intermediate Exercise should be a margin entry which reads [L/R Mar:0.5",0.5"]. This code was entered when the new left and right margins were created. L/R Mar: indicates that this is a left and right margin setting. The first 0.5" sets the left margin at one-half inch. The second, 0.5" sets the right margin at one-half inch.

The second entry is the base font entry [Font:Line Printer 16.67cpi]. This code was entered when the base font of the document was changed. Line Printer identifies that the line printer typeface will be used and that it prints 16.67 characters per inch. [Center] is the code that causes the following text to be centered.

The final code on the first line of the text is [HRt]. This is a hard return that indicates the end of a paragraph. It was created by pressing the <ENTER> key. The end of a line that is not the end of a paragraph is represented by [SRt]. WordPerfect inserts a soft return when it performs an automatic word wrap. Other codes found in this document are [TabSet:...] indicating tab settings, [Tab] denoting a tab stop, and [Dec Tab] signifying alignment on a decimal tab.

Displayed codes can be deleted. When the cursor is moved around the screen, it stops at each code as well as at each character. The codes can be erased by highlighting the code and pressing the Delete key.

1. Using the arrow keys, highlight the code [Center] on the first line of the document displayed on the bottom half of the screen.

Highlight: [Center]

2. To delete the center code, press the Del key.

Press: Del key

The screen displays

```
COMPUTER PRICE LIST
                              September 5, 1995

VS-Model 2              640K RAM     two 3.5"     portable     1,299.00
VSC-159-12              640K RAM     two 5.25"    desktop      1,349.00
VSC-286-25              512K RAM     20M hard     desktop      1,899.00
VSF-386-40              1M RAM       40M hard     desktop      3,399.00

NOTES:                  These computers are IBM-comptible and include MS-DOS.
                        have color monitors except the portable.  All computer
                        carry-in warranty.
A:\PRICES                                      Doc 1 Pg 1 Ln 1" Pos 0.5"
{    ▲    ▲    ▲    ▲    ▲    ▲    ▲    ▲    ▲    ▲    ▲    ▲    ▲    ▲    }
[L/R Mar:0.5",0.5"][Font:Line Printer 16.67cpi]COMPUTER PRICE LIST[HRt]
[Center]September 5, 1995[HRt]
[HRt]
[Tab Set:Rel: -0.5",+2.6",+4",+5.3",+7.1"]VS[-]Model 2[Tab]640K RAM[Tab]two 3.5"
[Tab]portable[Dec Tab]1,299.00[HRt]
VSC[-]159[-]12[Tab]640K RAM[Tab]two 5.25"[Tab]desktop[Dec Tab]1,349.00[HRt]
VSC[-]286[-]25[Tab]512K RAM[Tab]20M hard[Tab]desktop[Dec Tab]1,899.00[HRt]
VSF[-]386[-]40[Tab]1M RAM[Tab]40M hard[Tab]desktop[Dec Tab]3,399.00[HRt]
[HRt]
NOTES:[→Indent]These computers are IBM[-]comptible and include MS[-]DOS.  All of

Press Reveal Codes to restore screen
```

The heading COMPUTER PRICE LIST is no longer centered on the screen because the centering code was deleted.

3. To reinsert the centering code, press the Shift-F6 key combination and press the down arrow key.

Press: Shift-F6
Press: down arrow key

The [Center] code is inserted and the text is centered.

4. To turn off the Reveal Codes screen, press the Alt-F3 key combination.

Press: Alt-F3

This altered document will not be saved.

5. To clear this file from the screen, select the Exit option by pressing the F7 key. Indicate that the document is not to be saved by typing N, and remain in WordPerfect by typing N.

Press: F7
Type: N
Type: N

Master Documents

When a large document such as a book or an annual report is being created, it can be divided into separate files for each chapter or major topic. Shorter files are easier to edit and can be edited by multiple parties. Later, these separate files (subdocuments) can be printed as a single document using a master document.

A file containing a letterhead can be created and saved and then printed at the top of any document by inserting the letterhead as a subdocument. A subdocument can be placed anywhere within a master document.

A master document is any file containing subdocuments. Subdocuments are added to a master document by positioning the cursor at the location of the subdocument insertion, selecting Mark Text, indicating the Subdocument option, and typing the subdocument's file name.

When the subdocument is entered into the master document, a message indicating the location of the subdocument is displayed on the screen. This message can be expanded to display the entire subdocument. The subdocument can be edited either while expanded in the master document or as a separate document. To print the master document and all of the subdocuments as a single document, the subdocuments must be expanded.

To create a master document containing the PAPER and BIBLIOG files, complete the following steps.

Verify: cursor at top of document

1. Verify that the cursor is positioned at the top of the document.

Press: Alt-F5

2. To begin inserting a subdocument, press the Alt-F5 key combination.

   The bottom of the screen displays

   ```
   1 Auto Ref; 2 Subdoc; 3 Index; 4 ToA Short Form; 5 Define; 6 Generate: 0
   ```

Type: 2

3. To select Subdocument, type 2.

   The bottom of the screen displays

   ```
   Subdoc Filename:
   ```

Type: A:PAPER
Press: <ENTER>

4. To indicate the file PAPER, type A:PAPER and press <ENTER>.

   The screen displays

   ```
   Subdoc: A:PAPER

   Doc 1 Pg 1 Ln 1" Pos 1"
   ```

5. To begin inserting the second subdocument, press the Alt-F5 key combination.

   The bottom of the screen displays

   `1 Auto Ref; 2 Subdoc; 3 Index; 4 ToA Short Form; 5 Define; 6 Generate: 0`

   Press: Alt-F5

6. To select Subdocument, type 2.

   The bottom of the screen displays

   `Subdoc Filename:`

   Type: 2

7. To indicate the file BIBLIOG, type A:BIBLIOG and press <ENTER>.

   The top of the screen displays

Subdoc: A:PAPER

Subdoc: A:BIBLIOG

   Type: A:BIBLIOG
   Press: <ENTER>

8. To expand the subdocuments, press the Alt-F5 key combination.

   The bottom of the screen displays

   `1 Auto Ref; 2 Subdoc; 3 Index; 4 ToA Short Form; 5 Define; 6 Generate: 0`

   Press: Alt-F5

9. To Generate the expanded document, type 6.

   The screen displays

```
Mark Text: Generate

     1 - Remove Redline Markings and Strikeout Text from Document

     2 - Compare Screen and Disk Documents and Add Redline and Strikeout

     3 - Expand Master Document

     4 - Condense Master Document

     5 - Generate Tables, Indexes, Cross-References, etc.




Selection: 0
```

   Type: 6

Type: 3

10. To Expand the Master Document, type 3.

The screen displays

```
Subdoc Start: A:PAPER

     Stealing is running rampant in our schools, colleges, and
universities under the guise of software piracy.  The illegal
copying of software poses large, difficult, emotional, and
philosophical questions.  Some observers even think this common
practice of stealing software is endangering our ethics. [9, p.
181]  There must be an increase in societal awareness of the mutual
obligations of computer software users and developers.
     What a computer program is determines how the law can and will
protect it.  Therefore, before viewing the kinds of legal
protection accorded software, a basic understanding of what
constitutes a computer program is desirable.
     A computer program is a set of instructions which tells the
computer how to do its work.  Several steps are involved in writing
a program.  First the issues to be handled must be identified and
formulated.  Next a solution in the form of an algorithm must be
clearly expressed usually with the aid of a flow chart.  The flow
chart is used as a guide for putting the algorithm in computer
language which is known as code.  Once the program has been written
in code, it becomes a source program and can be translated by a
compiler into machine language.  When expressed in machine
                                        Doc 1 Pg 1 Ln 1" Pos 1"
```

The message and the box surrounding the message do not print.

Press: PgDn key

11. Scroll down through the document by pressing the PgDn key until the end of the PAPER file is displayed.

The screen displays

```
public opposition to piracy as a moral issue will be sufficient to
bring the problem under control." [7, p. 239]  Although the current
laws are unclear, I feel that educators have a moral obligation to
refrain from pirating software and to discourage others from doing
so in the classroom and at the work place.  Students need to be
educated as to the ethical and economic implications of such a
practice.

Subdoc End: A:PAPER

Subdoc Start: A:BIBLIOG

                    Selected Bibliography

1.   Adams, J. Mack, and Haden, Douglas H.  Social Effects of
     Computer Use and Misuse.  New York: John Wiley & Sons, 1976.

2.   Breslow, Jordan J.  "Caveats for Custom Software." PC-World,
     March 1985, pp.227-235.

3.   Bunnell, David.  "Software Piracy--One More Time."  PC-World,
                                        Doc 1 Pg 4 Ln 3.67" Pos 1"
```

The master document is ready to be saved. When a master document is saved, WordPerfect provides the option of saving each of the subdocuments. These additional saves need to be made if any changes have occurred to the subdocuments while the master document was being edited or created.

To save the master document using the filename MASTER, complete the following steps.

1. To save the document, press the F10 key.

   Press: F10

   The bottom of the screen displays

   `Document is expanded, condense it? Yes (No)`

2. The master document will consume more disk space if it is saved in its expanded mode. To save it in the condensed mode, type Y.

   Type: Y

   The bottom of the screen displays

   `Save Subdocs? Yes (No)`

3. As we have made no changes in the subdocuments, they need not be saved. To avoid saving the subdocuments, type N.

   Type: N

   The bottom of the screen displays

   `Document to be saved:`

4. To save the file on drive A: and to indicate MASTER as the filename, type A:MASTER.

   Type: A:MASTER

5. To execute the Save command, press <ENTER>.

   Press: <ENTER>

Footnotes

Footnotes are entered on separate footnote screens and are printed automatically at the bottom of the appropriate pages. Once the location of the footnote reference is determined, the footnote is created by placing the cursor at the location of the footnote, pressing the Ctrl-F7 key combination, entering the text of the footnote, and pressing the F7 key to exit the footnote option. The footnotes are automatically numbered and entered into the document.

To enter a footnote into the MASTER document, complete the following steps.

1. The MASTER document is on the screen in compressed form. Expand the master document by pressing the Alt-F5 key combination, typing 6, and typing 3.

   Press: Alt-F5
   Type: 6
   Type: 3

2. Position the cursor in the first paragraph of the document at the end of the sentence **Some observers even think this common practice of stealing software is endangering our ethics**.

   Position Cursor: at end of sentence

   A reference note, [9, p. 181], is found at the end of this entry and will be replaced by a complete footnote.

Press: Ctrl-F7

3. To begin the footnote, press the Ctrl-F7 key combination.

   The bottom of the screen displays

   `1 Footnote; 2 Endnote; 3 Endnote Placement: 0`

   Notice that this option can be used to create endnotes by selecting Endnote instead of Footnote.

Type: 1

4. To select the Footnote option, type 1.

   The bottom of the screen displays

   `Footnote: 1 Create; 2 Edit; 3 New Number; 4 Options: 0`

Type: 1

5. To create a footnote, type 1.

   The screen displays

```
    1








Footnote:  Press Exit when done                    Doc 1 Pg 1 Ln 1.5" Pos 1.56"
```

   The highlighted 1 indicates that this footnote will be numbered 1.

Type: underlined text as shown at right

6. To enter the text for the footnote, type Lewenstein, Bruce V. "The Ethics of Software Piracy." PC Magazine, April 30, 1985, p. 181..

   The footnote entry is made in the same manner that text is entered into the document. All of the editing tools available in normal text entry are available in footnote entry.

Press: F7

7. To enter the footnote, press the F7 key.

   A highlighted 1 has been entered at the cursor's location indicating the location of the footnote just created.

Indexing

WordPerfect can be used to create an index and a table of contents for a document. The text that is to appear in an index or a table of contents is marked within the document using the Mark Text option to indicate whether it is an index or a table of contents entry.

A location for the index or table of contents file must be specified before WordPerfect can create an index or a table of contents. The cursor is positioned at the location for the index or table of contents, and the define feature is selected from the Mark Text options.

After the entries for an index/table of contents have been identified, and the location for the index/table of contents file defined, the entries must be generated. This is done by selecting the Generate feature from the Mark Text menu and specifying whether to make new tables, indexes, or a table of contents.

In this exercise, an index will be created. A table of contents could be created by following the same procedures and substituting the Table of Contents options for the Index options.

To create an index for the MASTER file, complete the following steps.

1. Position the cursor at the **s** in the phrase **software piracy** that appears at the end of the first sentence in the document.

   The phrase **software piracy** is to be added to the document's index.

   Position cursor: at the s in software piracy

2. To turn Block on, press the Alt-F4 key combination.

   Press: Alt-F4

3. Use the right arrow key to highlight the phrase **software piracy**.

   Highlight: software piracy

4. To mark the text as an index entry, press the Alt-F5 key combination.

   Press: Alt-F5

   The bottom of the screen displays

   `Mark for: 1 ToC; 2 List; 3 Index; 4 ToA: 0`

5. To select the Index option, type 3.

   Type: 3

   The bottom of the screen displays

   `Index heading: Software piracy`

6. To accept Software piracy as the heading, press <ENTER>.

   Press: <ENTER>

   The bottom of the screen displays

   `Subheading:`

Press:	<ENTER>	7. To indicate no subheading, press <ENTER>. WordPerfect returns to the edit mode.
Position cursor:	at the s in software piracy	8. Position the cursor at the **s** in the phrase **software piracy** which appears in the first sentence of the eighth paragraph which begins **In an effort to cut down on software piracy.** The phrase software piracy is to be added to the document's index a second time.
Press:	Alt-F4	9. To turn Block on, press the Alt-F4 key combination.
Highlight:	software piracy	10. Use the right arrow key to highlight the phrase **software piracy**.
Press:	Alt-F5	11. To mark the text as an index entry, press the Alt-F5 key combination. The bottom of the screen displays `Mark for: 1 ToC; 2 List; 3 Index; 4 ToA: 0`
Type:	3	12. To select the Index option, type 3. The bottom of the screen displays `Index heading: Software piracy`
Press:	<ENTER>	13. To accept **Software piracy** as the heading, press <ENTER>. The bottom of the screen displays `Subheading:`
Press:	<ENTER>	14. To indicate no subheading, press <ENTER>. WordPerfect returns to the edit mode.
Position cursor:	under the f in freeware/shareware	15. Position the cursor on the letter **f** in **freeware/shareware** which appears in the first sentence of the sixteenth paragraph, beginning **The second category of software is.**
Press:	Alt-F5	16. To mark the word as an index entry, press the Alt-F5 key combination. The bottom of the screen displays `1 Auto Ref; 2 Subdoc; 3 Index; 4 ToA Short Form; 5 Define; 6 Generate: 0` Because this index entry is a single word, it need not be blocked before being marked.

17. To indicate an index entry, type 3. | **Type:** 3

The bottom of the screen displays

```
Index heading: Freeware/shareware
```

18. To accept **Freeware/shareware** as the heading, press <ENTER>. | **Press:** <ENTER>

The bottom of the screen displays

```
Subheading:
```

19. To indicate no subheading, press <ENTER>. | **Press:** <ENTER>

WordPerfect returns to the edit mode.

To save time, we will assume that all of the desired words have been marked for inclusion in the index. Next, the location of the index in the MASTER file is indicated and the index is generated.

To finish the process of building an index, complete the following steps.

1. To position the cursor at the end of the document, press the Home key twice followed by the down arrow key. | **Press:** Home key twice | **Press:** down arrow key

   The cursor moves to the end of the document.

2. To mark this spot as the location for the index, press the Alt-F5 key combination. | **Press:** Alt-F5

   The bottom of the screen displays

```
1 Auto Ref; 2 Subdoc; 3 Index; 4 ToA Short Form; 5 Define; 6 Generate: 0
```

3. To Define an index, type 5. | **Type:** 5

   The screen displays

```
Mark Text: Define

     1 - Define Table of Contents

     2 - Define List

     3 - Define Index

     4 - Define Table of Authorities

     5 - Edit Table of Authorities Full Form




Selection: 0
```

Type: 3	4. To select Define Index, type 3.

The screen displays

```
Concordance Filename (Enter=none):
```

The Concordance Filename requested by WordPerfect is another tool that can be used when creating indexes. A concordance file is not used in this exercise.

Press: <ENTER>

5. To continue defining the index, press <ENTER>.

The screen displays

```
Index Definition

     1 - No Page Numbers

     2 - Page Numbers Follow Entries

     3 - (Page Numbers) Follow Entries

     4 - Flush Right Page Numbers

     5 - Flush Right Page Numbers with Leaders


Selection: 5
```

Type: 2

6. To select the Page Numbers Follow Entries option, type 2.

WordPerfect returns to the edit mode.

Press: Alt-F5

7. To begin index generation, press the Alt-F5 key combination.

The bottom of the screen displays

```
1 Auto Ref; 2 Subdoc; 3 Index; 4 ToA Short Form; 5 Define; 6 Generate: 0
```

Type: 6

8. To select Generate, type 6.

The screen displays

```
Mark Text: Generate

     1 - Remove Redline Markings and Strikeout Text from Document

     2 - Compare Screen and Disk Documents and Add Redline and Strikeout

     3 - Expand Master Document

     4 - Condense Master Document

     5 - Generate Tables, Indexes, Cross-References, etc.


Selection: 0
```

9. To select Generate Tables, Indexes, etc., type 5. | **Type:** 5

The bottom of the screen displays

```
Existing tables, lists, and indexes will be replaced.  Continue? Yes (No)
```

10. To replace existing tables, etc., type Y. | **Type:** Y

The index is displayed at the end of the document and WordPerfect returns to the edit mode.

Windows

Checking for identical terminology in separate files or moving a block of text from one file to another file can be difficult. The Window command is used to divide the screen into two parts, allowing for the simultaneous display of two separate files. The monitor acts as a window through which various portions of the text can be viewed. The cursor can be switched back and forth between the two windows. The window containing the cursor is the active window and can be edited. Changes made in one window do not affect the text in the other window.

To copy text from one window to another, the screen command is activated by pressing the Ctrl-F3 key combination. The Window option is selected and the size of the window specified. The cursor is positioned in the new window, the second document is loaded, and the text to be moved is blocked. The blocked text is saved in memory. The cursor is moved to the first window and positioned where the text is to be inserted. Finally, the block of text is retrieved.

To place the paragraph in the PARAGRAF file into the MASTER document, complete the following steps.

1. To activate the screen command, press the Ctrl-F3 key combination. | **Press:** Ctrl-F3

   The bottom of the screen displays

```
1 Window; 2 Line Draw; 3 Rewrite: 3
```

2. To select the Window option, type 1. | **Type:** 1

   The screen displays

```
Number of lines in this window: 24
```

3. To split the screen in half, type 12 and press <ENTER>. | **Type:** 12 **Press:** <ENTER>

   The screen is split in two. The top half contains the MASTER document and the bottom half is empty.

Press: Shift-F3	4. To activate the bottom half of the screen, press the Shift-F3 key combination. The cursor moves to the bottom half of the screen.
Press: Shift-F10	5. To retrieve the PARAGRAF file, press the Shift-F10 key combination. The bottom of the screen displays `Document to be retrieved:`
Type: A:PARAGRAF **Press:** <ENTER>	6. To indicate the PARAGRAF file, type A:PARAGRAF and press <ENTER>. The PARAGRAF file is displayed on the bottom half of the screen.
Press: Alt-F4	7. To turn Block on, press the Alt-F4 key combination. The bottom of the screen flashes `Block on`.
Press: down arrow key	8. Highlight the paragraph by pressing the down arrow key. (The end of the file may extend past the bottom of the screen.)
Press: F10	9. To save the marked block to memory, press the F10 key. The bottom of the screen displays `Block name:`
Press: <ENTER>	10. To save the block to memory, press <ENTER> without naming the block.
Press: Shift-F3	11. To move the cursor to the upper document, press the Shift-F3 key combination.
Position cursor: at the beginning of the second paragraph	12. Using the arrow keys, position the cursor at the beginning of the second paragraph, **What a computer program is determines how the law can and will protect it.**
Press: Shift-F10	13. To retrieve the block of text, press the Shift-F10 key combination. The bottom of the screen displays `Document to be retrieved:`
Press: <ENTER>	14. To indicate the block in memory, press <ENTER> without providing a document name. The paragraph is inserted into the document.

15. To close the bottom window, press the Ctrl-F3 key combination.

Press: Ctrl-F3

The bottom window displays

`0 Rewrite; 1 Window; 2 Line Draw: 0`

16. To select the Window option, type 1.

Type: 1

The bottom of the screen displays

`Number of lines in this window: 12`

17. To close the window, type 30 (or any number larger than the number of lines that your screen can display, for most screens this is 24) and press <ENTER>.

Type: 30
Press: <ENTER>

The bottom window disappears.

Saving a Document and Exiting WordPerfect

To save all of the changes made to this document, including the index and the added paragraph, and to exit from WordPerfect, complete the following steps.

1. To begin the save and exit process, press the F7 key.

Press: F7

The bottom of the screen displays

`Save document? Yes (No)`

2. To indicate Yes, press <ENTER>.

Press: <ENTER>

The bottom of the screen displays

`Document is expanded, condense it? Yes (No)`

If the master document is saved in expanded mode, the file will consume additional space. A good practice is to condense a document before saving.

3. To condense the document, press <ENTER>.

Press: <ENTER>

The bottom of the screen displays

`Save Subdocs? Yes (No)`

The Subdocuments have been changed and should be saved.

4. To save the subdocuments, press <ENTER>.

Press: <ENTER>

The screen displays:

`Replace A:PAPER? 1 Yes; 2 No; 3 Replacd All Remaining: 0`

Type: 3

5. To save and replace all of the subdocuments, type 3.

   After several messages briefly appear, the bottom of the screen displays

   `Document to be saved: A:MASTER`

Press: <ENTER>

6. To save the MASTER document, press <ENTER>.

   The bottom of the screen displays

   `Replace      A:MASTER? No (Yes)`

Type: Y

7. To replace the existing MASTER file, type Y.

   The screen displays

   `Exit doc 1?  No (Yes)`

Type: Y

8. To close the MASTER document (doc 1), type Y.

   The paragraph document is still open as a second document and is displayed on the screen. Closing the window on this document earlier in the exercise did not close the document. The document remained open as document number 2.

Press: F7

9. To exit from WordPerfect, press the F7 key.

   The bottom of the screen displays

   `Save document? Yes (No)`

Press: N

10. To skip saving the document, type N.

    The bottom of the screen displays

    `Exit WP? No (Yes)          (Cancel to return to document)`

Type: Y

11. To Exit from WordPerfect, type Y.

The system prompt (C>, a menu, or something similar) is displayed on the screen.

Conclusion

Through the Beginning, Intermediate, and Advanced Exercises, some of the features of WordPerfect have been explored. Hundreds of other functions exist which far exceed the level of expertise addressed in these lessons. Further information on additional WordPerfect features can be obtained from the WordPerfect manual.

1. Practice:
   Loading WordPerfect
   Font Types
   Footnotes
   Viewing a Document in Printed Form
   Printing a Document
   Exiting WordPerfect

   a. Load WordPerfect as described in the Loading WordPerfect section of the Beginning Word Perfect Exercise.

   b. Type the following paragraph:

      The Font command can be used to create superscripts and subscripts and to vary font styles and sizes. The font choices will vary depending upon the printer in use. The following examples were created on a Hewlett-Packard LaserJet Series II printer using only the standard fonts.

   c. Using the arrow keys, position the cursor under the first character of the paragraph.

   d. To view the document as it would appear on the printed page, press the Shift-F7 key combination followed by a 6.

   e. To return to the editing mode, press the F7 key.

   f. Change the current font and activate the Font command by pressing the Ctrl-F8 key combination.

   g. To select the Base Font option, type 4.

   h. Use the arrow keys to select a font smaller than the current font. On a dot matrix printer, a good choice would be compressed type. On an inkjet printer or laser printer, the line printer font (16.66 pitch) would be a good choice.

   i. To activate the font, press <ENTER>.

   j. To examine how the document will look in the smaller typeface, press the Shift-F7 key combination followed by a 6.

   k. The reformatted paragraph is displayed on the screen.

   l. To return to edit mode, press the F7 key.

   m. Using the arrow keys, position the cursor immediately after the end of the second sentence in the paragraph. This will mark the location of a footnote.

   n. Begin the footnote creation process by pressing the Ctrl-F7 key combination.

   o. Type 1 to select a footnote.

   p. Enter the following text for the footnote:

      This is a footnote for the above paragraph.

   q. To enter the footnote, press the F7 key.

   r. A highlighted 1 has been entered at the cursor's location, indicating the location of the footnote.

   s. To examine how the document will look in the smaller typeface with the footnote, press the Shift-F7 key combination followed by a 6.

   t. The paragraph is displayed on the screen.

   u. To return to edit mode, press the F7 key.

   v. Print the document by pressing the Shift-F7 key combination followed by a 1.

   w. Exit WordPerfect by pressing the F7 key and replying N to the "Save Document?" question.

2. Practice:
   Loading WordPerfect
   Master Documents
   Indexing
   Printing a Document
   Exiting WordPerfect

   This exercise uses the COVER, BODY, and TABLE1 files created in the Intermediate WordPerfect practice exercises. These files should reside on a diskette in drive A:.

   a. Load WordPerfect as described in the Loading WordPerfect section of the Beginning WordPerfect Exercise.

   b. Create a master document consisting of the COVER, BODY, and TABLE1 files. Begin this process by pressing the Alt-F5 key combination.

   c. Select Subdocument by typing 2.

   d. To indicate the file COVER, type A:COVER <ENTER>.

   e. Press the Alt-F5 key combination and select Subdocument by typing 2.

   f. Type A:BODY and press <ENTER> to create the second subdocument.

   g. Press the Alt-F5 key combination and select Subdocument by typing 2.

   h. Type A:TABLE1 and press <ENTER> to create the third subdocument.

   i. Expand the subdocuments by pressing the Alt-F5 key combination.

   j. Generate the expanded document by typing 6.

   k. Scroll through the document, using the arrow keys, and note the location of each of the subdocuments.

   l. Select several topics in the BODY section of the document and create an index for them. Begin the indexing process by using the arrow keys to position the cursor at the first letter of the first phrase to be indexed and press the Alt-F4 key combination.

   m. Highlight the phrase to be indexed by using the right arrow key.

   n. Mark the phrase selected as an index entry by pressing the Alt-F5 key combination.

   o. Select an Index option by typing 3.

   p. Accept the displayed phrase by pressing <ENTER>.

   q. Indicate no subheadings by pressing <ENTER>.

   r. Repeat steps (l.) through (q.) two more times to create a total of three index items.

   s. Using the arrow keys, position the cursor at the end of the document and press <ENTER> twice to create two blank lines.

   t. Mark this spot as the location of the index by pressing the Alt-F5 key combination.

   u. Define an Index by typing 5.

   v. Select Define Index by typing 3 and pressing <ENTER>.

   w. To select the Page Numbers Follow Entries option, type 2.

   x. To begin the index generation, press the Alt-F5 key combination.

   y. Select Generate by typing 6.

   z. Select Generate Tables, Indexes, etc. by typing 5 and replace existing tables by typing Y. The index is displayed at the end of the document.

   aa. Exit WordPerfect by pressing the F7 key and replying N to the "Save Document?" question.

3. Practice:
   Loading WordPerfect
   Font Types
   Footnotes
   Viewing a Document in Printed Form
   Printing a Document
   Exiting WordPerfect

   a. Load WordPerfect as described in the Loading WordPerfect section of the Beginning Word Perfect Exercise.

   b. Type the following paragraph:

      In general, the computer has two disk drives. This can be two floppy disk drives or one floppy disk drive and one hard disk drive. For a two-floppy disk drive machine, the drive on the left or top is drive A: and the drive on the right or bottom is drive B:. Usually, a diskette containing the operating system (MS-DOS) is placed in drive A:. For a hard disk drive machine, the floppy disk drive is drive A: and the hard disk drive is drive C:. Usually, the operating system is on the hard disk drive and no diskette is needed to boot the system.

   c. Using the arrow keys, position the cursor under the first character of the paragraph.

   d. To view the document as it would appear on the printed page, press the Shift-F7 key combination followed by a 6.

   e. To return to the editing mode, press the F7 key.

   f. Change the current font and activate the Font command by pressing the Ctrl-F8 key combination.

   g. To select the Base Font option, type 4.

   h. Use the arrow keys to select a font smaller than the current font. On a dot matrix printer, a good choice would be compressed type. On an inkjet printer or laser printer, the line printer font (16.66 pitch) would be a good choice.

   i. To activate the font, press <ENTER>.

   j. To examine how the document will look in the smaller typeface, press the Shift-F7 key combination followed by a 6.

   k. The reformatted paragraph is displayed on the screen.

   l. To return to edit mode, press the F7 key.

   m. Using the arrow keys, position the cursor immediately after the end of the second sentence in the paragraph. This will mark the location of a footnote.

   n. Begin the footnote creation process by pressing the Ctrl-F7 key combination.

   o. Type 1 to select a footnote.

   p. Enter the following text for the footnote:

      This is a footnote for the above paragraph.

   q. To enter the footnote, press the F7 key.

   r. A highlighted 1 has been entered at the cursor's location, indicating the location of the footnote.

   s. To examine how the document will look in the smaller typeface with the footnote, press the Shift-F7 key combination followed by a 6.

   t. The paragraph is displayed on the screen.

   u. To return to edit mode, press the F7 key.

   v. Print the document by pressing the Shift-F7 key combination followed by a 1.

   w. Exit WordPerfect by pressing the F7 key and replying N to the "Save Document?" question.

4. Practice:
   Loading WordPerfect
   Master Documents
   Indexing
   Printing a Document
   Exiting WordPerfect

   This exercise uses the COVER2, BODY2, and TABLE2 files created in the Intermediate WordPerfect practice exercises. These files should reside on a diskette in drive A:.

   a. Load WordPerfect as described in the Loading WordPerfect section of the Beginning WordPerfect Exercise.

   b. Create a master document consisting of the COVER2, BODY2, and TABLE2 files. Begin this process by pressing the Alt-F5 key combination.

   c. Select Subdocument by typing 2.

   d. To indicate the file COVER2, type A:COVER2 <ENTER>.

   e. Press the Alt-F5 key combination and select Subdocument by typing 2.

   f. Type A:BODY2 and press <ENTER> to create the second subdocument.

   g. Press the Alt-F5 key combination and select Subdocument by typing 2.

   h. Type A:TABLE2 and press <ENTER> to create the third subdocument.

   i. Expand the subdocuments by pressing the Alt-F5 key combination.

   j. Generate the expanded document by typing 6.

   k. Scroll through the document, using the arrow keys and noting the location of each of the subdocuments.

   l. Select several topics in the BODY2 section of the document and create an index for them. Begin the indexing process by using the arrow keys to position the cursor at the first letter of the first phrase to be indexed and press the Alt-F4 key combination.

   m. Highlight the phrase to be indexed by using the right arrow key.

   n. Mark the phrase selected as an index entry by pressing the Alt-F5 key combination.

   o. Select an Index option by typing 3.

   p. Accept the displayed phrase by pressing <ENTER>.

   q. Indicate no subheadings by pressing <ENTER>.

   r. Repeat steps (l.) through (q.) two more times to create a total of three index items.

   s. Using the arrow keys, position the cursor at the end of the document, and press <ENTER> twice to create two blank lines.

   t. Mark this spot as the location of the index by pressing the Alt-F5 key combination.

   u. Define an Index by typing 5.

   v. Select Define Index by typing 3 and pressing <ENTER>.

   w. To select the Page Numbers Follow Entries option, type 2.

   x. To begin the index generation, press the Alt-F5 key combination.

   y. Select Generate by typing 6.

   z. Select Generate Tables, Indexes, etc. by typing 5 and replace existing tables by typing Y. The index is displayed at the end of the document.

   aa. Exit WordPerfect by pressing the F7 key and replying N to the "Save Document?" question.

5. Practice:
   Loading WordPerfect
   Font Types
   Footnotes
   Viewing a Document in Printed Form
   Printing a Document
   Exiting WordPerfect

   a. Load WordPerfect as described in the Loading WordPerfect section of the Beginning Word Perfect Exercise.

   b. Type the following paragraph:

      Floppy disks fail no matter how expensive they are and no matter how carefully they are handled. The read/write heads of the disk drive come into physical contact with the disk surface. This contact eventually wears out the magnetic surface of the diskette. When this happens, data and programs stored in the worn area are lost.

   c. Using the arrow keys, position the cursor under the first character of the paragraph.

   d. To view the document as it would appear on the printed page, press the Shift-F7 key combination followed by a 6.

   e. To return to the editing mode, press the F7 key.

   f. Change the current font and activate the Font command by pressing the Ctrl-F8 key combination.

   g. To select the Base Font option, type 4.

   h. Use the arrow keys to select a font smaller than the current font. On a dot matrix printer, a good choice would be compressed type. On an inkjet printer or laser printer, the line printer font (16.66 pitch) would be a good choice.

   i. To activate the font, press <ENTER>.

   j. To examine how the document will look in the smaller typeface, press the Shift-F7 key combination followed by a 6.

   k. The reformatted paragraph is displayed on the screen.

   l. To return to edit mode, press the F7 key.

   m. Using the arrow keys, position the cursor immediately after the end of the second sentence in the paragraph. This will mark the location of a footnote.

   n. Begin the footnote creation process by pressing the Ctrl-F7 key combination.

   o. Type 1 to select a footnote.

   p. Enter the following text for the footnote:

      This is a footnote for the above paragraph.

   q. To enter the footnote, press the F7 key.

   r. A highlighted 1 has been entered at the cursor's location, indicating the location of the footnote.

   s. To examine how the document will look in the smaller typeface with the footnote, press the Shift-F7 key combination followed by a 6.

   t. The paragraph is displayed on the screen.

   u. To return to edit mode, press the F7 key.

   v. Print the document by pressing the Shift-F7 key combination followed by a 1.

   w. Exit WordPerfect by pressing the F7 key and replying N to the "Save Document?" question.

6. Practice:
   Loading WordPerfect
   Master Documents
   Indexing
   Printing a Document
   Exiting WordPerfect

   This exercise uses the COVER3, BODY3, and TABLE3 files created in the Intermediate WordPerfect practice exercises. These files should reside on a diskette in drive A:.

   a. Load WordPerfect as described in the Loading WordPerfect section of the Beginning WordPerfect Exercise.

   b. Create a master document consisting of the COVER3, BODY3, and TABLE3 files. Begin this process by pressing the Alt-F5 key combination.

   c. Select Subdocument by typing 2.

   d. To indicate the file COVER, type A:COVER3 <ENTER>.

   e. Press the Alt-F5 key combination and select Subdocument by typing 2.

   f. Type A:BODY2 and press <ENTER> to create the second subdocument.

   g. Press the Alt-F5 key combination and select Subdocument by typing 2.

   h. Type A:TABLE3 and press <ENTER> to create the third subdocument.

   i. Expand the subdocuments by pressing the Alt-F5 key combination.

   j. Generate the expanded document by typing 6.

   k. Scroll through the document, using the arrow keys and noting the location of each of the subdocuments.

   l. Select several topics in the BODY3 section of the document and create an index for them. Begin the indexing process by using the arrow keys to position the cursor at the first letter of the first phrase to be indexed and press the Alt-F4 key combination.

   m. Highlight the phrase to be indexed by using the right arrow key.

   n. Mark the phrase selected as an index entry by pressing the Alt-F5 key combination.

   o. Select an Index option by typing 3.

   p. Accept the displayed phrase by pressing <ENTER>.

   q. Indicate no subheadings by pressing <ENTER>.

   r. Repeat steps (l.) through (q.) two more times to create a total of three index items.

   s. Using the arrow keys, position the cursor at the end of the document, and press <ENTER> twice to create two blank lines.

   t. Mark this spot as the location of the index by pressing the Alt-F5 key combination.

   u. Define an Index by typing 5.

   v. Select Define Index by typing 3 and pressing <ENTER>.

   w. To select the Page Numbers Follow Entries option, type 2.

   x. To begin the index generation, press the Alt-F5 key combination.

   y. Select Generate by typing 6.

   z. Select Generate Tables, Indexes, etc. by typing 5 and replace existing tables by typing Y. The index is displayed at the end of the document.

   aa. Exit WordPerfect by pressing the F7 key and replying N to the "Save Document?" question.

1. Using WordPerfect, create a paragraph that includes underlined, bold, and compressed print. Display the paragraph on the screen as it would be printed. Display the formatting codes, remove the compressed print code, and display the paragraph on the screen as it would be printed.

2. Using the file created in practice exercise #3 of the WordPerfect Intermediate Exercise, add a minimum of 5 footnotes to the document. Paginate the document and display it on the screen as it would be printed. Change the line spacing from double spacing to single spacing and redisplay it on the screen as it would be printed. Print the document single-spaced. Save the document on disk.

3. Using the file created in practice exercise #2 above, identify 15 terms in the document to be included in an index and mark them appropriately. Create an index for the document immediately following the title page. Display the document on the screen as it would be printed, including the index. Save the document with the index on disk. Print the document.

4. Use the file created in practice exercise #3 above. Add a table of contents, save the file, and print the document.

5. Create three documents with the file names: BODY, TABLE, and LIST. The BODY file should be a two-page document consisting of only text. The TABLE file should consist of a list of seven people containing each person's name, city, state, age, and sex in a column format. The LIST file should be a one-column list consisting of local restaurants. Create and save a master document called WHOLE, containing the TABLE file, followed by the BODY file, followed by the LIST file. Print the document with page numbers centered at the bottom of each page, with the first page number appearing on the second page. Neither the table nor the list should be split between pages.

6. Using the file WHOLE, created in practice exercise #5 above, add two footnotes to the text portion of the document. Then, print the entire document.

7. Use WordPerfect to create a letterhead for your personal use.

8. Use WordPerfect to create a letterhead for your professional use.

9. Use WordPerfect to create a letterhead for a pet shop.

10. Copy the PAPER file on the Exercise Disk to your working data disk. Print an index of at least forty entries indentified in the software piracy document.

11. Copy the PAPER file on the Exercise Disk to your working data disk. Print a table of contents of entries indentified in the software piracy document.

12. Write a one-page, double-spaced paper indicating the font types supported by your computer printer.

13. Retrieve the PRICES file created in the WordPerfect Intermediate Exercise. Save the document with a new filename called MYPRICES. Reformat the document so that the NOTES: section at the bottom of the price list extends from the left margin to the right margin rather than being indented.

14. Retrieve the PRICES file created in the WordPerfect Intermediate Exercise. Save the document with a new filename called MYPRICES2. Insert your professional letterhead created in practice exercise #8 above at the top of this price list. Change the date of the price list to reflect the current month and year. Print the document.

15. Copy the PAPER file on the Exercise Disk to your working data disk. Save the document with a new file name called MYPAPER. Use a global search and replace to

change the word **authors** to **writers**, and the word **hardware** to **equipment**.

16. Scan the WordPerfect manual. Use WordPerfect to create and print a two-page, double-spaced paper indicating five additional word processing features that you would like to explore.

17. Use WordPerfect to create and print a three-page, double-spaced document that discusses at what age a child should learn keyboarding skills.

18. Incorporating various font styles, use WordPerfect to create and print a church bulletin.

19. Incorporating various font styles, use WordPerfect to create and print a concert/theatre program.

20. Use WordPerfect to produce a research paper. Include a table of contents and a bibliography.

WordPerfect 5.1
Spell Checking and Thesaurus Exercise

Objectives

Learn how to:

1. Electronically spell check a document and correct the misspelled words.
2. Add a word to WordPerfect's spelling checker dictionary.
3. Use the thesaurus to select synonyms for a word.

Scope of the Exercise

This lesson describes how to use the spell checking and thesaurus features of WordPerfect. This includes finding and correcting misspelled words, adding new words to WordPerfect's dictionary, and using the thesaurus to select alternative words.

Starting the Lesson

For this lesson, everything to be typed at the keyboard is underlined and also appears in the margin. Text appearing on the computer's screen during the lesson is shown in `courier type`.

1. Before the WordPerfect program can be used to turn a computer into a word processor, the operating system must be loaded into the computer. If a system prompt (C>, a menu, or something similar) is not displayed on the screen, follow the steps described in the Getting Started Exercise in the DOS module to boot the system.

   Boot: the computer

2. If you are using a hard drive system and the WordPerfect installation instructions have been followed, WordPerfect resides on the hard drive. Insert a formatted diskette into drive A:. The diskette in drive A: is the working data disk. Any files created during this lesson will be saved onto this disk.

   Insert: data disk in drive A:

   -or-

   If a computer with a different configuration is being used, ask your instructor or lab assistant for directions specific to your setup.

Loading WordPerfect

The computer must be provided with instructions on how to be a word processor. This is done by loading the WordPerfect program into the computer's temporary memory (RAM). To load WordPerfect and to begin executing the program, complete the following steps.

Type: CD\WP51
Press: <ENTER>
Type: WP

1. If you are using a hard drive, log into the WordPerfect subdirectory by typing CD\WP51 and pressing <ENTER>. Then, type WP.

   -or-

   If you are in a lab or network setting, verify the above commands with your instructor or lab assistant.

Press: <ENTER>

2. Execute the above command by pressing the <ENTER> key. The Enter key signals to the computer that the command has been typed and needs to be carried out.

Spell Checking a Document

The spelling checker for WordPerfect can check words on a single page or throughout an entire document. Words can be added to the WordPerfect spelling checker dictionary. In addition, the WordPerfect spelling checker can provide suggested spellings for identified misspelled words.

Three steps are required to check and correct the spelling of an existing document. First, the spell checking menu line is displayed. Second, the spell checking option is selected and the first word not recognized by WordPerfect is highlighted. Third, the appropriate word or action is chosen from the menu. Once the action is selected, the cursor moves to the next misspelled word.

To activate the spell checking option to correct the sentence **Thes is a teast of the spell cheker**, complete the following steps.

Type: Thes is a teast of the spell cheker.

1. Enter the sentence to be checked by typing Thes is a teast of the spell cheker.

Press: Ctrl-F2

2. Activate the spell checking option by pressing the Ctrl-F2 key combination.

   The bottom of the screen displays

```
Check: 1 Word; 2 Page; 3 Document; 4 New Sup. Dictionary; 5 Look Up; 6 Count: 0
```

3. To check the entire document (in this case, a single sentence), type 3.

Type: 3

The cursor highlights the word **Thes** and the screen displays

```
Thes is a teast of the spell cheker




                                                   Doc 1 Pg 1 Ln 1" Pos 1"
{   ▲   ▲   ▲   ▲   ▲   ▲   ▲   ▲   ▲   ▲   ▲   ▲   }   ▲   ▲

  A. tees                 B. the                  C. thee
  D. them                 E. then                 F. these
  G. thews                H. they                 I. this
  J. thus                 K. ties                 L. toes
  M. tues                 N. thais                O. thaws
  P. theist               Q. thighs               R. those


Not Found: 1 Skip Once; 2 Skip; 3 Add; 4 Edit; 5 Look Up; 6 Ignore Numbers: 0
```

The three columns below the line of triangles contain WordPerfect's guesses as to the correct spelling of the highlighted word. Any of these words can be selected to replace the highlighted word by typing its corresponding letter.

The message line at the bottom of the screen indicates that the highlighted word was Not Found in WordPerfect's dictionary and offers 5 options. The first two options are used to avoid spell checking the highlighted word. **Skip Once** indicates skip this word at this time but highlight it again if it is found later. **Skip** indicates not to highlight this word as misspelled during this spell checking session. The **Add** option adds the highlighted word to WordPerfect's permanent dictionary. When this addition has been made, this word will not be highlighted as being misspelled in any WordPerfect document. The **Edit** option is used to manually correct the highlighted word. The **Look Up** option is used to look up words in the dictionary with WordPerfect's look up patterns. The final option, **Ignore Numbers**, is used to tell WordPerfect to ignore numbers when checking spelling.

Type: I

4. To replace **Thes** with the correct word **This**, type I.

   Thes is replaced with **This**. The cursor highlights the word **teast** and the screen displays

```
This is a teast of the spell cheker




                                                   Doc 1 Pg 1 Ln 1" Pos 2"
{   ▲   ▲   ▲   ▲   ▲   ▲   ▲   ▲   ▲   ▲   ▲   ▲   }   ▲   ▲

  A. teart                  B. teas                  C. tease
  D. teat                   E. teats                 F. test
  G. toast                  H. east                  I. ptosed
  J. tacet                  K. tacit                 L. tacite
  M. taoist                 N. taste                 O. tasted
  P. teased                 Q. testate               R. teste
  S. tested                 T. testoid               U. theist
  V. thiazide               W. toasted               X. tossed
Press Enter for more words

Not Found: 1 Skip Once; 2 Skip; 3 Add; 4 Edit; 5 Look Up; 6 Ignore Numbers: 0
```

   The line **Press Enter for more words** indicates that all of WordPerfect's guesses do not fit on the screen. Fortunately, the desired spelling is displayed. If it were not, pressing the <ENTER> key would display more choices.

Type: F

5. To select the correct word, **test**, type F.

   Teast is replaced by **test**. The cursor highlights the work **cheker** and the screen displays

```
This is a test of the spell cheker




                                                   Doc 1 Pg 1 Ln 1" Pos 3.8"
{   ▲   ▲   ▲   ▲   ▲   ▲   ▲   ▲   ▲   ▲   ▲   ▲   }   ▲   ▲

  A. checker                B. cheer                 C. chewer
  D. choker                 E. calker                F. caulker
  G. chalkier               H. chaucer               I. cheekier
  J. choicer                K. chukker               L. coacher
  M. coaxer                 N. cocker                O. cockier
  P. cooker                 Q. coucher               R. kicker
  S. kickier                T. kookier


Not Found: 1 Skip Once; 2 Skip; 3 Add; 4 Edit; 5 Look Up; 6 Ignore Numbers: 0
```

6. To replace **cheker** with the correct word, **checker**, type A.

   Type: A

   The bottom of the screen displays

```
Word count: 8          Press any key to continue
```

7. To continue, press the space bar.

   Press: space bar

   The space bar is a good key to use when the computer displays "press any key." The space bar is large and is not likely to cause serious problems if it is accidentally pressed more than once.

Using the Thesaurus

A thesaurus is used to look up synonyms. When writing a document you may find yourself using the same word over and over again. Both you and your reader will tire of repetitive words. A thesaurus is used to look up word alternatives. Usually, a thesaurus is a book.

WordPerfect has a built-in thesaurus. To use the thesaurus, position the cursor at the word in question and activate the Thesaurus option by pressing the Alt-F1 key combination. WordPerfect displays synonyms grouped by word usage, such as by verb and noun categories. To replace the word in question, type the letter appearing next to the desired alternative word.

To use the thesaurus to look up synonyms for the word **test**, complete the following steps.

1. Position the cursor on the word **test** by pressing the left arrow key.

   Position cursor: on test

2. To activate the thesaurus, press the Alt-F1 key combination.

   Press: Alt-F1

   The screen displays

```
This is a test of the spell checker


test=(n)
 1 A  comprehensive   |      ·verify        |
   B ·examination     |                     |
   C ·final           | 5    ·analyze       |
   D ·quiz            |      ·inspect       |
   E ·review          |      ·investigate   |
                      |      ·probe         |
 2 F ·essay           |                     |
   G ·experiment      | 6    ·examine       |
   H ·trial           |      ·question      |
                      |      ·quiz          |
 3 I ·analysis        |---------------------|
   J ·inquiry         |                     |
   K ·investigation   |                     |
                      |                     |
test-(v)--------------|                     |
 4 L ·check           |                     |
   M ·prove           |                     |
   N ·try             |                     |
1 Replace Word; 2 View Doc; 3 Look Up Word; 4 Clear Column: 0
```

Four options appear in the bottom line menu. Replace Word is selected to replace the word in question with one of the words on the list. View Doc is used to scroll through the document to look for other words. The Look Up Word option is used to look up any word in the thesaurus by typing it in. The Clear Column option clears a column of word options from the screen.

Only the words in the left column of word choices are accompanied by a letter. No other words may be selected. The left and right arrow keys are used to display letters for words in other columns.

For the word **test**, WordPerfect is able to find several words that are nouns and several that are verbs. These are indicated by (n) and (v). Suggested synonyms are displayed by meaning in numbered groups on the screen. There are three meaning categories under both the noun and verb groups for the word **test**.

Typing the corresponding letter of one of the words causes the synonyms for that word to be displayed on the screen.

Type: E

3. To display the synonyms for **review**, type E.

The screen displays

```
This is a test of the spell checker



test=(n)=====================  review=(n)==========================================
 1    comprehensive             1 A ·analysis                      ·evaluate
      ·examination                B ·commentary
      ·final                      C  evaluation              5     reassess
      ·quiz                                                        reevaluate
      ·review                   2 D ·examination                   reexamine
                                  E  reassessment
 2    ·essay                      F  reevaluation
      ·experiment                 G ·scrutiny
      ·trial                      H ·study

 3    ·analysis                 3 I ·journal
      ·inquiry                    J ·magazine
      ·investigation              K ·periodical
                                  L ·publication
test-(v)---------------------
 4    ·check                   review-(v)------------------
      ·prove                    4 M ·criticize
      ·try                        N ·critique
1 Replace Word; 2 View Doc; 3 Look Up Word; 4 Clear Column: 0
```

The first column containing synonyms for **test** remains on the screen while the other column is replaced with two columns for the word **review**.

The first word listed for **review** is **analysis**. This word meets our needs.

4. To replace the word **test**, type 1. — **Type:** 1

   The bottom of the screen displays

   `Press letter for word`

5. To select **analysis**, type A. — **Type:** A

   Test is replaced with the word **analysis**.

Exiting WordPerfect

To exit WordPerfect, complete the following steps.

1. To exit WordPerfect, press the F7 key. — **Press:** F7

   The bottom of the screen displays

   `Save document? Yes (No)`

2. To avoid saving the document, type N. — **Type:** N

   The bottom of the screen displays

   `Exit WP? No (Yes)          (Cancel to return to document)`

3. To exit WordPerfect, type Y. — **Type:** Y

   The system prompt (C>, a menu, or something similar) is displayed on the screen.

Conclusion

WordPerfect has excellent spell checking and thesaurus capabilities. Every writer should use these capabilities if only to find occasional typing errors! Spell checking does not identify the misuse of a correctly spelled word. It merely indicates words not contained in the spell checking dictionary.

Practice Using Spell Checking and the Thesaurus

1. Add your family name to WordPerfect's spelling checker dictionary.

2. Retrieve the PAPER file from the Exercise Disk. Use WordPerfect's spelling checker to check the spelling of this document.

3. Retrieve the PAPER file from the Exercise Disk. Use WordPerfect's thesaurus to find alternative words for complex, protest, and believe. The search and replace feature can be used to quickly locate these words. Save the edited file with the file name PAPERSPL.

4. Retrieve the PAPER file from the Exercise Disk. Use WordPerfect's spelling checker to count the number of words in this document.

5. Add ten acronyms, terms, and/or proper nouns used frequently in your writing to a new supplemental WordPerfect dictionary.

WordPerfect 5.1
Mail Merge

Objectives

Learn how to:

1. Describe the process of mail merging.

2. Recognize potential mail merge applications.

3. Define and use the following terms:

   variable label
   export
   mail merge
   template

Defining Mail Merge

Word processing not only provides the means of producing an error-free document quickly and easily, but it also provides a means of producing hundreds of personalized documents. Text created with a word processor can be merged with the information listed in a data base. Bringing together the variable data from a data base with the fixed information of a word-processed document is accomplished through the process of mail merging.

Mail merge applications abound in education and in business. Some potential uses include: mailings of employment agreements, contracts, employee benefit statements, class schedules, new product lines, price updates, and schedule reminders. Mail merge technology has the capability of personalizing a "Dear Friend" form letter. In the past, it was not economically feasible to produce large volumes of individualized letters manually.

Using mail merge, productivity gains are enormous. A typical word processing program with mail merge capabilities using a high-speed laser printer is capable of producing 500 one-page letters per hour. Each of these letters looks as though it were personally (and perfectly) typed.

For example, a library needs to notify individuals that books are overdue. The information regarding the overdue books is in a data base.

Sample library data base:

Lastname	Firstname	Title	Street	City	State	Books
Smith	John	Mr.	12 Maple St.	Holt	MI	3
Doe	Harry	Mr.	123 Park Ave.	Paris	MI	1
Williams	Kathy	Mrs.	110 Hilltop Rd.	Shelby	MI	2
.						
.						
.						

A letter is written to the borrowers. Each letter includes a name, an address, and the number of overdue books. When merging a letter with a data base, all of the fields in the data base need not be used in the text of the letter.

Sample mail merge letter:

March 1, 1995

Firstname Lastname
Street
City, State

Dear *Title Lastname*,

It has come to our attention that you have *Books* overdue books from this library. You are requested to return these books immediately or be subject to library fines. Please note that this is not an April Fool's prank.

Sincerely,

John C. Vonsnockendorfer
Library Collection Agency

Notice that in place of the actual names, variable labels (shown in italics) appear. These labels represent fields from the data base.

The names and addresses from the library data base file are retrieved from disk. This data is merged with the text of the letter. The appropriate information for each person is inserted in place of the variable label indicated in the text. The information kept on every person borrowing books is maintained and updated with the editing capabilities of the data base software. The letter is retained with other letters and can be modified as needs change.

The following mail merge exercise uses the WordPerfect word processor and a data file in DIF format that could have come from any data base management program. DIF stands for Data Interchange Format and is often used to transfer data between programs. Before the data can be used by the word processor, it must be transferred to a format recognized by WordPerfect.

WordPerfect 5.1
Mail Merge Exercise

Objectives

Learn how to:

1. Convert a data base data file to WordPerfect format.

2. Create a mail merge template in WordPerfect.

3. Print merged letters using WordPerfect.

Scope of the Exercise

This lesson describes how to load and use the data base conversion program that comes with WordPerfect and the word processing program WordPerfect 5.1 to mail merge a letter. The topics covered include: converting a file, creating a mail merge template, and printing a mail merge document.

The Mail Merge Process

Mail merge is the process of joining information contained in a data base with a document created by a word processor. The mail merge process consists of three steps: creating the data file, creating the merge document, and joining the data base with the merge document.

In this exercise, the following steps will be taken to join information from a **CHARACTR** data base file with a letter created in WordPerfect:

a. Load the WordPerfect **CONVERT** program,
b. Convert the data file to a WordPerfect secondary file format,
c. Load WordPerfect,
d. Create the letter primary merge file in WordPerfect; and
e. Perform the merge operation.

The secondary file contains the name and address information that is to be joined with the text of the letter. The data in the secondary file must be in a format unique to WordPerfect. The primary merge file contains the text of the letter to be sent to all of the people in the data file and the positions where the data from the secondary file are to be located.

The mail merge process can be used in the business community to send letters to current customers informing them of new products or services. A club or organization can use the mail merge process to send newsletters to members. Using mail merge, each letter can be personally addressed and customized.

Starting the Lesson

For this lesson, everything to be typed at the keyboard is <u>underlined</u> and also appears in the margin. Text appearing on the computer's screen during the lesson is indicated in `courier type`.

Boot: the computer

1. Before the WordPerfect program can be used to turn a computer into a word processor, the operating system must be loaded into the computer. If a system prompt (C>, a menu, or something similar) is not present on the screen, follow the steps described in the Getting Started Exercise in the DOS module to boot the system.

Copy: CHARACTR.DIF file onto data disk

2. One data file has been created for use with this exercise. Copy the file CHARACTR.DIF from the Exercise Disk provided with this module onto a formatted disk. This disk will be the working data disk.

Insert: data disk in drive A:

3. If you are using a hard drive system and the WordPerfect installation instructions have been followed, WordPerfect resides on the hard drive. Insert a working data diskette containing the above file into drive A:. Any files created during this lesson also will be saved onto this disk.

   -or-

   If a computer with a different configuration is being used, ask your instructor or lab assistant for directions specific to your setup.

Converting Files to a WordPerfect Format

The CHARACTR.DIF file must be converted to a WordPerfect secondary merge format before it can be used in this exercise. The data file could be created with WordPerfect. However, WordPerfect is not a data base management program and maintaining a mailing list with WordPerfect can be difficult. A data base manager organizes information for mailing lists more effectively. Therefore, for illustrative purposes in this exercise, a data base file has been prepared for use with WordPerfect. A WordPerfect program called **CONVERT** is used to convert foreign file formats into WordPerfect secondary merge format.

Loading the CONVERT Program

The computer must be provided with the instructions on how to convert one file format into another. This is done by loading the WordPerfect conversion program into the computer's temporary memory (RAM). To load the CONVERT program and to begin executing the program, complete the following steps.

1. If you are using a hard drive system, log into the WordPerfect subdirectory by typing CD\WP51 and pressing <ENTER>. Verify that the working data diskette containing the CHARACTR.DIF file is in drive A: and type convert.

   Type: CD\WP51
   Press: <ENTER>

   Type: convert

   -or-

   If you are in a lab setting, ask your instructor or lab assistant for directions specific to your setup.

Convert is the command that tells MS-DOS to load the WordPerfect convert program into the computer and to start the program.

2. Execute the above command by pressing the <ENTER> key. The Enter key signals to the computer that the command has been typed and needs to be carried out.

   Press: <ENTER>

   The screen momentarily displays

```
WordPerfect
 Conversion
  Utility

   5.1

(C) Copyright 1984, 1989
  All Rights Reserved
WordPerfect Corporation
   Orem, Utah  USA
```

   Then the screen displays

```
Name of Input File?
```

Converting the File

The conversion process is not complicated. After the CONVERT program has been executed, the input and output files are indicated and a conversion option is selected from the displayed menu.

To convert the CHARACTR.DIF file, complete the following steps.

Type: a:charactr.dif
Press: <ENTER>

1. To indicate the CHARACTR.DIF file on drive A: as the input file, type a:charactr.dif and press <ENTER>.

   The screen displays

```
Name of Input File? a:charactr.dif
Name of Output File?
```

Type: a:charactr.mrg
Press: <ENTER>

2. To indicate an output file on drive A: having the name of CHARACTR.MRG, type a:charactr.mrg and press <ENTER>.

   The screen displays

```
Name of Input File? a:charactr.dif
Name of Output File? a:charactr.mrg


0 EXIT
1 WordPerfect to another format
2 Revisable-Form-Text (IBM DCA Format) to WordPerfect
3 Final-Form-Text (IBM DCA Format) to WordPerfect
4 Navy DIF Standard to WordPerfect
5 WordStar 3.3 to WordPerfect
6 MultiMate Advantage II to WordPerfect
7 Seven-Bit Transfer Format to WordPerfect
8 WordPerfect 4.2 to WordPerfect 5.1
9 Mail Merge to WordPerfect Secondary Merge
A Spreadsheet DIF to WordPerfect Secondary Merge
B Word 4.0 to WordPerfect
C DisplayWrite to WordPerfect

Enter number of Conversion desired
```

Type: a

3. To select Spreadsheet DIF to WordPerfect Secondary Merge, type A.

   The file is converted and the screen displays

```
Name of Input File? a:charactr.dif
Name of Output File? a:charactr.mrg


0 EXIT
1 WordPerfect to another format
2 Revisable-Form-Text (IBM DCA Format) to WordPerfect
3 Final-Form-Text (IBM DCA Format) to WordPerfect
4 Navy DIF Standard to WordPerfect
5 WordStar 3.3 to WordPerfect
6 MultiMate Advantage II to WordPerfect
7 Seven-Bit Transfer Format to WordPerfect
8 WordPerfect 4.2 to WordPerfect 5.1
9 Mail Merge to WordPerfect Secondary Merge
A Spreadsheet DIF to WordPerfect Secondary Merge
B Word 4.0 to WordPerfect
C DisplayWrite to WordPerfect

Enter number of Conversion desired A
a:charactr.dif Converted to a:charactr.mrg
```

Note the system prompt at the bottom of the screen, which indicates that control of the system has been returned to the operating system.

Loading WordPerfect

The computer must be provided with the instructions on how to be a word processor. This is done by loading the WordPerfect program into the computer's temporary memory (RAM). To load WordPerfect and to begin executing the program, complete the following steps.

1. If you are using a hard drive, log into the WordPerfect subdirectory by typing CD\WP51 and pressing <ENTER>. Then, type WP. (Uppercase or lowercase may be used.)

   Type: cd\wp51
   Type: <ENTER>
   Type: wp

   -or-

   If you are in a lab or network setting, verify the above commands with your instructor or lab assistant.

2. Execute the above command by pressing the <ENTER> key. The Enter key signals to the computer that the command has been typed and needs to be carried out.

   Press: <ENTER>

   The Return key and Enter key, if the keyboard has both, are interchangeable. These lessons will use <ENTER> to indicate that either the Return key or Enter key is to be pressed.

Creating a Document for Mail Merging

The Secondary File

The secondary file is the CHARACTR.MRG file. This file contains the data that is to be merged into a letter. It will be loaded into memory so that it may easily be examined during the creation of the primary file.

To load the secondary data file, CHARACTR.MRG, into WordPerfect, complete the following steps.

1. To retrieve the CHARACTR.MRG file, press the Shift-F10 key combination.

   Press: Shift-F10

   The bottom of the screen displays

   ```
   Document to be retrieved:
   ```

Type: a:charactr.mrg
Press: <ENTER>

2. To indicate CHARACTR.MRG on drive A:, type a:charactr.mrg and press <ENTER>.

   The screen displays

```
LASTNAME{END FIELD}
FIRSTNAME{END FIELD}
TITLE{END FIELD}
STREET{END FIELD}
CITY{END FIELD}
STATE{END FIELD}
ZIP{END FIELD}
AMOUNT{END FIELD}
SEX{END FIELD}
BIRTHDAY{END FIELD}
HOBBIES{END FIELD}
{END RECORD}
Charming{END FIELD}
Prince{END FIELD}
Mr.{END FIELD}
42 Wanderlust Lane{END FIELD}
Forest Grove{END FIELD}
MN{END FIELD}
55555{END FIELD}
10.00{END FIELD}
M{END FIELD}
12/05/27{END FIELD}
riding, singing, jousting{END FIELD}
{END RECORD}
Field: 1                                        Doc 1 Pg 1 Ln 1" Pos 1"
```

   The records to be merged are displayed. Each record is separated by {END RECORD}. Each field is listed on a separate line and is followed by {END FIELD}. If a particular field is empty, an {END FIELD} appears by itself. The first record displayed consists of the field names. This is because the DIF file format was used to transfer the data from a data base program to WordPerfect. When the data file and letter file are merged, a letter will be created containing the field names. However, the presence of the field names makes the creation of the primary document easier.

The Primary File

The next step in the mail merge process is to create the primary document. The primary document consists of an output template. The output template is the model of the document to be printed. The field number is included with the {FIELD} merge codes to indicate the field to be used in the primary document. When the primary document is merged with the secondary file and then printed, the information represented by the {FIELD} numbers will appear in place of the field codes.

In a merge template, all of the fields included in the secondary file need not be used in the output template. The fields may be used more than once and they can be placed in any sequence.

If the primary document is a letter, the field numbers representing the name and address information are placed where the inside address is to appear. The greeting is inserted by indicating the field numbers for the title and last name. Then, the body of the letter is typed.

To create a primary document, complete the following steps.

1. To Switch to a second document, press the Shift-F3 key combination.

   Type: Shift-F3

   A blank second document and the message, `Doc 2 Pg 1 Ln 1" Pos 1"`, are displayed on the screen.

2. To display both documents on the screen, press the Ctrl-F3 key combination.

   Press: Ctrl-F3

   The bottom of the screen displays

   ```
   1 Window; 2 Line Draw; 3 Rewrite: 3
   ```

3. To select the `Window` option, type 1.

   Type: 1

   The bottom of the screen displays

   ```
   Number of lines in this window: 24
   ```

4. To change the number to 12, type 12 and press <ENTER>.

   Type: 12
   Press: <ENTER>

   The screen displays

   ```
   LASTNAME{END FIELD}
   FIRSTNAME{END FIELD}
   TITLE{END FIELD}
   STREET{END FIELD}
   CITY{END FIELD}
   STATE{END FIELD}
   ZIP{END FIELD}
   AMOUNT{END FIELD}
   SEX{END FIELD}
   BIRTHDAY{END FIELD}
   Field: 1                                   Doc 1 Pg 1 Ln 1" Pos 1"
   {  ▼  ▼  ▼  ▼  ▼  ▼  ▼  ▼  ▼  ▼  ▼  ▼  }  ▼  ▼




                                              Doc 2 Pg 1 Ln 1" Pos 1"
   ```

5. To enter the date at the left margin, type March 1, 1995 and press <ENTER>.

   Type: March 1, 1995
   Press: <ENTER>

6. Space down to the inside address location by pressing the <ENTER> key twice.

   Press: <ENTER> twice

Press: Shift-F9

7. To begin entering the merge code for the **TITLE** field, press the <u>Shift-F9</u> key combination.

   The bottom of the screen displays

```
1 Field; 2 End Record; 3 Input; 4 PageOff; 5 Next Record; 6 More:
0
```

Type: 1

8. To select Field, type <u>1</u>.

   The bottom of the screen displays

```
Field:
```

   WordPerfect is requesting the field number. This is determined by looking at the top half of the screen and counting. The **LASTNAME** field is number one. Counting down shows that the **TITLE** field is number three.

Type: 3
Press: <ENTER>

9. To insert field three at the cursor location, type <u>3</u> and press <u><ENTER></u>.

   The screen displays

```
LASTNAME{END FIELD}
FIRSTNAME{END FIELD}
TITLE{END FIELD}
STREET{END FIELD}
CITY{END FIELD}
STATE{END FIELD}
ZIP{END FIELD}
AMOUNT{END FIELD}
SEX{END FIELD}
BIRTHDAY{END FIELD}
Field: 1                                          Doc 1 Pg 1 Ln 1" Pos 1"
{   ▾   ▾   ▾   ▾   ▾   ▾   ▾   ▾   ▾   ▾   ▾   ▾   }   ▾   ▾
March 1, 1995


{FIELD}3~






                                              Doc 2 Pg 1 Ln 1.5" Pos 1.2"
```

Press: space bar

10. To place a space between the **TITLE** field and the **FIRSTNAME** field, press the <u>space bar</u>.

Press: Shift-F9

11. To begin entering the merge code for the **FIRSTNAME** field, press the <u>Shift-F9</u> key combination.

   The bottom of the screen displays

```
1 Field; 2 End Record; 3 Input; 4 PageOff; 5 Next Record; 6 More: 0
```

12.	To select Field, type 1. The bottom of the screen displays `Field:`	**Type:** 1
13.	To insert field two, **FIRSTNAME**, at the cursor location, type 2 and press <ENTER>.	**Type:** 2 **Press:** <ENTER>
14.	To place a space between the **FIRSTNAME** field and the **LAST-NAME** field, press the space bar.	**Press:** space bar
15.	To begin entering the merge code for the **LASTNAME field, press the** Shift-F9 key combination. The bottom of the screen displays `1 Field; 2 End Record; 3 Input; 4 PageOff; 5 Next Record; 6 More: 0`	**Press:** Shift-F9
16.	To select Field, type 1. The bottom of the screen displays `Field:`	**Type:** 1
17.	To insert field one, **LASTNAME**, at the cursor location; type 1 and press <ENTER>.	**Type:** 1 **Press:** <ENTER>
18.	To move the cursor to the next line, press <ENTER>.	**Press:** <ENTER>
19.	To begin entering the merge code for the **STREET** field, press the Shift-F9 key combination.	**Press:** Shift-F9
20.	To select Field, type 1.	**Type:** 1
21.	To insert field four, **STREET**, at the cursor location, type 4 and press <ENTER>.	**Type:** 4 **Press:** <ENTER>
22.	To move the cursor to the next line, press <ENTER>.	**Press:** <ENTER>
23.	To begin entering the merge code for the **CITY** field, press the Shift-F9 key combination.	**Press:** Shift-F9
24.	To select Field, type 1.	**Type:** 1
25.	To insert field five, **CITY**, at the cursor location, type 5 and press <ENTER>.	**Type:** 5 **Press:** <ENTER>
26.	To insert a comma and a space after the **CITY** field, type , (a comma) and press the space bar.	**Type:** , **Press:** space bar
27.	To begin entering the merge code for the **STATE** field, press the Shift-F9 key combination.	**Press:** Shift-F9

Type:	1	28. To select Field, type 1.
Type: **Press:**	6 <ENTER>	29. To insert field six, **STATE**, at the cursor location; type 6 and press <ENTER>.
Press:	space bar	30. To insert a space after the **STATE** field, press the space bar.
Press:	Shift-F9	31. To begin entering the merge code for the **ZIP** field, press the Shift-F9 key combination.
Type:	1	32. To select Field, type 1.
Type: **Press:**	7 <ENTER>	33. To insert field seven, **ZIP**, at the cursor location; type 7 and press <ENTER>.
Press:	<ENTER> twice	34. To insert a blank line, press <ENTER> twice.
Type:	Dear (with a space after the r)	35. To begin the salutation, type Dear . Be sure to include the space following the r.
Press:	Shift-F9	36. To begin entering the merge code for the **TITLE** field, press the Shift-F9 key combination.
Type:	1	37. To select Field, type 1.
Type: **Press:**	3 <ENTER>	38. To insert field three, **TITLE**, at the cursor location, type 3 and press <ENTER>.
Press:	space bar	39. To insert a blank space, press the space bar.
Press:	Shift-F9	40. To begin entering the merge code for the **LASTNAME** field, press the Shift-F9 key combination.
Type:	1	41. To select Field, type 1.
Type: **Press:**	1 <ENTER>	42. To insert field one, **LASTNAME**, at the cursor location, type 1 and press <ENTER>.
Type:	:	43. To insert a colon, type : .

44. To insert a blank line, press <ENTER> twice.

The screen displays

```
LASTNAME{END FIELD}
FIRSTNAME{END FIELD}
TITLE{END FIELD}
STREET{END FIELD}
CITY{END FIELD}
STATE{END FIELD}
ZIP{END FIELD}
AMOUNT{END FIELD}
SEX{END FIELD}
BIRTHDAY{END FIELD}
Field: 1                                            Doc 1 Pg 1 Ln 1" POS 1"
{   ▼   ▼   ▼   ▼   ▼   ▼   ▼   ▼   ▼   ▼   ▼   ▼   ▼   }   ▼   ▼
March 1, 1995


{FIELD}3~ {FIELD}2~ {FIELD}1~
{FIELD}4~
{FIELD}5~, {FIELD}6~ {FIELD}7~


Dear {FIELD}3~ {FIELD}1~:



                                                 Doc 2 Pg 1 Ln 2.83" Pos 1"
```

Press: <ENTER> twice

45. To begin the body of the letter, type As you are a highly esteemed inhabitant of . Be sure to type the space following the word **of**.

Type: As you are a highly esteemed inhabitant of

46. To begin entering the merge code for the **CITY** field, press the Shift-F9 key combination.

Press: Shift-F9

47. To select Field, type 1.

Type: 1

48. To insert field five, **CITY**, at the cursor location, type 5 and press <ENTER>.

Type: 5
Press: <ENTER>

49. To complete the document, type the underlined material as shown below, allowing the text to automatically word wrap to the next line. Your text may not have the same line breaks as the displayed text.

As you are a highly esteemed inhabitant of {FIELD}5~, you have been semiautomatically selected to participate in a fabulous offer. We are making available to you the use of our new "Erase 'Em and Weep" uncommonly unfailing disk drive.

If after a two-week trial you decide to keep our product, you need only pay us the diminutive sum of $5.00 a week for five years. All major credit cards are accepted and financing is available.

Sincerely,

I. M. Snekee
Director of Promotions

Type: underlined material as shown at left

Press: F10

50. To save the primary document, press the F10 key.

    The bottom of the screen displays

    `Document to be saved:`

Type: a:letter
Press: <ENTER>

51. To save the document with the name of LETTER on drive A:, type A:LETTER and press <ENTER>.

Merging the Secondary File with the Letter

The final step in the mail merge process is to join the data base file with the letter. This is accomplished by accessing the Merge/Sort menu. From the merge menu, the merge option is selected and then the primary file name is indicated. Next, the secondary file name is indicated.

To merge the data base information (the secondary file) with the sales letter (the primary file), complete the following steps.

Press: Ctrl-F9

1. To activate the Merge/Sort menu, press the Ctrl-F9 key combination.

   The bottom of the screen displays

   `1 Merge; 2 Sort; 3 Convert Old Merge Codes: 0`

Type: 1

2. To select the Merge option, type 1.

   The bottom of the screen displays

   `Primary file:`

Type: a:letter
Press: <ENTER>

3. To indicate the LETTER file on drive A:, type A:LETTER and press <ENTER>.

   The bottom of the screen displays

   `Secondary file:`

4. To indicate the CHARACTR.MRG file on drive A:, type A:CHARACTR.MRG and press <ENTER>.

Type: a:charactr.mrg
Press: <ENTER>

The screen displays

```
LASTNAME{END FIELD}
FIRSTNAME{END FIELD}
TITLE{END FIELD}
STREET{END FIELD}
CITY{END FIELD}
STATE{END FIELD}
ZIP{END FIELD}
AMOUNT{END FIELD}
SEX{END FIELD}
BIRTHDAY{END FIELD}
Field: 1                                           Doc 1 Pg 1 Ln 1" Pos 1"
{   ▼   ▼   ▼   ▼   ▼   ▼   ▼   ▼   ▼   ▼   ▼   ▼   }   ▼   ▼
If after a two-week trial you decide to keep our product, you need
only pay us the diminutive sum of $5.00 a week for five years.  All
major credit cards are accepted and financing is available.

Sincerely,


I. M. Snekee
Director of Promotions



A:\LETTER                                      Doc 2 Pg 7 Ln 5.33" Pos 1"
```

Nothing appears to have happened. However, a look at the lower right corner of the screen reveals that the cursor is located on Page 7 (Pg 7).

5. To examine the merged document, press the PgUp key six times.

Press: PgUp six times

The screen displays

```
LASTNAME{END FIELD}
FIRSTNAME{END FIELD}
TITLE{END FIELD}
STREET{END FIELD}
CITY{END FIELD}
STATE{END FIELD}
ZIP{END FIELD}
AMOUNT{END FIELD}
SEX{END FIELD}
BIRTHDAY{END FIELD}
Field: 1                                           Doc 1 Pg 1 Ln 1" Pos 1"
{   ▼   ▼   ▼   ▼   ▼   ▼   ▼   ▼   ▼   ▼   ▼   ▼   }   ▼   ▼
March 1, 1995


{FIELD}3~ {FIELD}2~ {FIELD}1~
{FIELD}4~
{FIELD}5~, {FIELD}6~ {FIELD}7~


Dear {FIELD}3~ {FIELD}1~:


As you are a highly esteemed inhabitant of {FIELD}5~, you have been
A:\LETTER                                      Doc 2 Pg 1 Ln 1" Pos 1"
```

The merged letter displayed on the screen is the first letter and contains the template. Use the PgDn key to display the other five letters on the screen. Each letter has a different inside name and address. The first line of the body of the letter ends with different words depending upon the length of the city's name.

Printing the Merged Document

Now that the data file has been merged into the letter and is contained in the computer's memory, it can be printed. The entire document could be printed by pressing the Shift-F7 key combination to activate the print menu and then by typing 1 to select Full Document. In order to save paper, only one letter will be printed. This is accomplished by moving the cursor to the page containing the letter to be printed, activating the print menu by pressing the Shift-F7 key combination, and typing 2 to select Page.

To print the letter for Daisy Duck, complete the following steps.

Position cursor: in Daisy Duck letter using PgUp or PgDn key

1. Using the PgUp or PgDn key, position the cursor in the letter addressed to Daisy Duck.

   The screen displays

```
LASTNAME{END FIELD}
FIRSTNAME{END FIELD}
TITLE{END FIELD}
STREET{END FIELD}
CITY{END FIELD}
STATE{END FIELD}
ZIP{END FIELD}
AMOUNT{END FIELD}
SEX{END FIELD}
BIRTHDAY{END FIELD}
Field: 1                                              Doc 1 Pg 1 Ln 1" Pos 1"
{  ▼   ▼   ▼   ▼   ▼   ▼   ▼   ▼   ▼   ▼   ▼   ▼   }   ▼   ▼
March 1, 1995


Ms. Daisy Duck
111 Quacker Ave.
Big Rapids, MI 49307


Dear Ms. Duck:


As you are a highly esteemed inhabitant of Big Rapids, you have
A:\LETTER                                             Doc 2 Pg 4 Ln 1" Pos 1"
```

Press: Shift-F7

2. To activate the print menu, press the Shift-F7 key combination.

   The screen displays the Print Menu.

3. To select the Page option, type 2. — **Type:** 2

The following letter is printed

```
March 1, 1995

Ms. Daisy Duck
111 Quacker Ave.
Big Rapids, MI 49307

Dear Ms. Duck:

As you are a highly esteemed inhabitant of Big Rapids,
you have been semiautomatically selected to partici-
pate in a fabulous offer.  We are making available to
you the use of our new "Erase 'Em and Weep" uncommonly
unfailing disk drive.

If after a two-week trial you decide to keep our prod-
uct, you need only pay us the diminutive sum of $5.00
a week for five years.  All major credit cards are ac-
cepted and financing is available.

Sincerely,


I. M. Snekee
Director of Promotions
```

A personalized letter to Daisy Duck has been printed and awaits the signature of I. M. Snekee.

Ending the Lesson

The mail merge operation has been completed. To exit from WordPerfect, complete the following steps.

1. To exit from the letter document, press the F7 key. — **Press:** F7

   The bottom of the screen displays

   `Save document? Yes (No)`

2. To answer no, type N. — **Type:** n

   The screen displays

   ```
   Exit doc 2? No (Yes)     (Cancel to return to docu-
   ment)
   ```

3. To answer yes, type Y. — **Type:** y

   The cursor moves to document one on the top half of the screen.

Press: F7

4. To exit from the secondary document, press the F7 key.

   The screen displays

   `Save document? Yes (No)`

Type: n

5. To answer no, type N.

   The screen displays

   `Exit WP? No (Yes)`

Type: y

6. To answer yes, type Y.

   WordPerfect has been exited and the system prompt (C>, menu system, or something similar) is displayed on the screen.

Conclusion

WordPerfect can be used with the data files from many data base management programs to print mail-merged letters. Many of the data base management programs can be used to create and print mail-merged documents. However, when complex formatting or typeface selections are needed, the letter writing features of data base managers are inadequate.

1. Copy the SOCIETY.DIF data file on the Exercise Disk to your working data disk. Use this data base to mail merge a personalized letter containing the computer price list created in the WordPerfect Intermediate Exercise to each of the addresses listed in the data base.

2. Copy the SOCIETY.DIF data file and the BIBLIOG file on the Exercise Disk to your working data disk. Use this data base to mail merge a personalized letter containing the bibliography to each of the addresses listed in the data base. Indicate in your letter that the bibliography is a list of required readings for the following term.

3. After completing the data base module, create a data base with the names and addresses of twenty relatives. Mail merge this data base with a letter inviting these family members to a reunion the following summer.

4. Use WordPerfect to create a certificate of participation for a local fund-raising event. Mail merge the first and last names in the SOCIETY.DIF data file on the Exercise Disk into the certificate file and print five certificates.

5. Use a data base manager to create a data file and mail merge a letter to all church members informing them of the annual church meeting to be held at 8:00 P.M. on December 15, 1995. The letter should be sent to the head of each family. The letter should be sent by the pastor, Rev. Red Zinger.

6. Use a data base manager to create a data file and mail merge a letter to all church children informing them of a New Year's Eve Party to be held from 8:00 P.M. until beyond midnight on December 31, 1994. The letter should be sent by the youth group leaders, Bill and Marilyn Gofer.

7. Use a data base manager to create a data file and mail merge a letter to employees of the firm, inviting them and their families to a company picnic to be held on July 17, 1995, at Central Park, beginning at 2:00 P.M. The letter should be sent to the employee at his/her home address. The spouse (by name) should be invited to attend.

INDEX

accessing help screens 7
Advanced WordPerfect Exercise 63
Advanced WordPerfect Projects 89
Alt-F2 key combination 15
Alt-F3 key combination 68
Alt-F4 key combination 12
Alt-F5 key combination 70
Alt-F8 key combination 17
applications 3
arrow keys 10
authors *v*
Backspace key 7
Beginning Exercise 5
Beginning WordPerfect Projects 27
block 11
block deletion 14
block restoration 14
boilerplate 3
booting the computer 6, 29, 63, 91, 102
centering text 32
changing type styles 16
CONVERT program 101
converting files to WordPerfect format 102
converting the file 103
copying text 11, 12
creating a document 1
creating a document for mail merging 105
Ctrl-F2 key combination 92
Ctrl-F4 key combination 9, 12
dBASE IV *iii*
decimal tabs 33
define index 78
defining word processing 1
Del key 7
deleting a text block 14
deleting text 10, 45
document creation 1
document editing 2
document formatting 2
document printing 2, 18
document saving 17
editing 1
editing a document 2
END FIELD 106
End key 10
entering text 7
equipment requirements *iv*
erasing typing errors 7
exercise disk *iv*
exiting WordPerfect 19, 46, 80, 97
expanding master documents 72
F3 key 7
F7 key 19
F8 key 30
FIELD 106
font types 64
footer lines 39
footnotes 73
format codes 67
format command 30, 32, 38
formatting 1
formatting a document 2
FoxPro *iii*
generate tables 79
global search 44
global search and replace 44
header lines 39
Hobart, R. Dale *v*
Home key 10
indents 35
indexing 75
inserting text 11
Intermediate Exercise 29
Intermediate WordPerfect Projects 61
joining files 36
left tab 33
letterhead 70
line spacing 38
loading the CONVERT program 103
loading WordPerfect 6, 30, 64, 92, 104
Lotus 2.2 *iii*
mail merge 3, 99
mail merge exercise 101
mail merge process 101
Mail Merge Projects 117
margin command 30
marking text 11
master documents 69
merging the secondary file with the letter 112
move command 13
moving around the screen 9
moving text 11, 13
Octernaud, Sharon *v*
organization of series *iv*
page numbers 40
pagination 42
Paradox 3 *iii*
philosophy *iii*
Practice Advanced WordPerfect 83
Practice Beginning WordPerfect 20

Practice Intermediate WordPerfect	48
Practice Spell Checking and the Thesaurus	98
primary file	106
print options	38
printing	1
printing a document	2, 18
printing the merged document	114
ProComm Plus	*iii*
replacing text	15
restoring a text block	14
retrieving files	37
revising text	10
right tab	33
saving a document	17, 80
searching text	15
secondary file	105
series organization	*iv*
setup requirements	*iv*
Shift-F10 key combination	37, 65
Shift-F7 key combination	18, 65
Shift-F8 key combination	30, 31,33
spell checking	91
spell checking a document	92
Spell Checking and Thesaurus Exercise	91
spelling checkers	3
subdocuments	70
synonyms	4
Sytsma, Sidney	*v*
tab command	32
table of contents	*vi*
tabs	35
text block deletion	14
text format codes	67
text replacing	15
text searching	15
thesaurus	95
thesaurus features	91
thesauruses	3
type styles	16
undeleting text	45
using indents	35
using tabs	35
using the thesaurus	95
VP Planner	*iii*
windows	79
word processing applications	3
word wrap	7
WordPerfect 5.1	*iii*
WordStar 5.5	*iii*